the QUILTED home

LEISURE ARTS, INC.
Little Rock, Arkansas

EDITORIAL STAFF

Vice President and Editor-in-Chief: Sandra Graham Case
Executive Director of Publications: Cheryl Nodine Gunnells
Director of Designer Relations: Debra Nettles
Senior Publications Director: Susan White Sullivan
Editorial Director: Susan Frantz Wiles
Photography Director: Stephen Wilson
Senior Art Operations Director: Jeff Curtis
Licensed Product Coordinator: Lisa Truxton Curton

PRODUCTION
Managing Editor: Cheryl R. Johnson
Technical Editor: Lisa Lancaster
Senior Technical Writer: Frances Huddleston

EDITORIAL
Associate Editor: Kimberly L. Ross

ART
Art Publications Director: Rhonda Hodge Shelby
Art Imaging Director: Mark Hawkins
Art Category Manager: Lora Puls
Graphic Artists: Ashley Carozza, Dayle Cosh and Chad Brown
Photography Stylists: Christina Tiano Myers and Cassie Newsome
Staff Photographer: Russell Ganser
Publishing Systems Administrator: Becky Riddle
Publishing Systems Assistants: Clint Hanson, Myra S. Means, and Chris Wertenberger

BUSINESS STAFF

Publisher: Rick Barton
Vice President, Finance: Tom Siebenmorgen
Director of Corporate Planning and Development: Laticia Mull Dittrich
Vice President, Retail Marketing: Bob Humphrey
Vice President, Sales: Ray Shelgosh
Vice President, National Accounts: Pam Stebbins

Director of Sales and Services: Margaret Reinold
Vice President, Operations: Jim Dittrich
Comptroller, Operations: Rob Thieme
Retail Customer Service Managers: Sharon Hall and Stan Raynor
Print Production Manager: Fred F. Pruss

Softcover ISBN 1-57486-319-3

10   9   8   7   6   5   4   3   2   1

Want to make your home even cozier and more inviting than it already is? Then try making one of the 17 delightful quilts we've gathered for *The Quilted Home*. From a table runner to full-size bed quilts, you'll find an assortment of projects in styles sure to charm the traditional quilter, the whimsical quilter, and everyone in between! Even better — clear diagrams, easy-to-follow instructions, and full-color photographs make these quilts a joy to create. So settle down in your favorite chair, and pick out a quilt or two to make your home a little sweeter.

Table of Contents

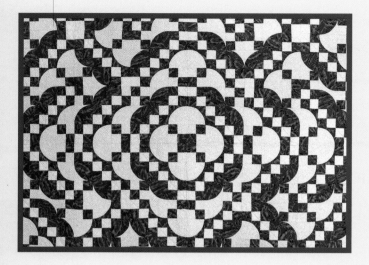

Jacob's Roller Coaster

QUILT BY LYN OSER MANN

Finished Size: 67" x 67" (170 x 170 cm)
Blocks: 36 – 9" (23 cm) Roller Coaster Blocks

As a new quilter, Lyn Oser Mann was fascinated with curved seams, but since she considers herself a strict traditionalist, the contemporary styles she saw didn't appeal to her. For fun, Lyn began experimenting with standard patterns by replacing straight seams with curved ones. *Jacob's Rollercoaster* was the result of trying this technique on the traditional Jacob's Ladder pattern.

Materials

4³/₈ yards (4 m) pink print
2¹/₂ yards (2.3 m) white-on-white print
1⁵/₈ yards (1.5 m) black for border and binding
4 yards (3.7 m) fabric for backing
Twin-size batting

Cutting

Measurements include ¹/₄" seam allowances. Cut crosswise strips unless otherwise noted. Follow *Rotary Cutting*, page 100. Patterns for B and C are on page 10.

From pink print, cut:
• 1 (2"-wide) strip. Trim strip into 1 (2" x 26") border corner strip.
• 18 (2"-wide) strips for A units.
• 9 (5"-wide) strips. Cut strips into 72 (5") squares. Cut each square into 1 B and 1 C.
• 1⁵/₈ yards. Cut yardage into 8 (3"-wide) lengthwise strips. Trim strips to make 8 (3" x 54¹/₂") border strips. From remainder, cut 2 (3" x 9") border corner strips.

From white-on-white print, cut:
• 18 (2"-wide) strips for A units.
• 9 (5"-wide) strips. Cut strips into 72 (5") squares. Cut each square into 1 B and 1 C.

From black, cut:
• 4 (2"-wide) lengthwise strips. Trim strips to make 4 (2" x 54¹/₂") border strips. From remainder, cut 1 (2" x 9") border corner strip.
• 1 (3"-wide) lengthwise strip. Cut strip into 2 (3" x 26") border corner strips.
• 5 (2¹/₄"-wide) lengthwise strips for binding.

Block Assembly

1. Join 1 white and 1 pink strip along long edges to make 1 strip set (*Strip Set A Diagram*). Make 18 strip sets. Cut strip sets into 360 (2"-wide) segments.

Strip Set A Diagram

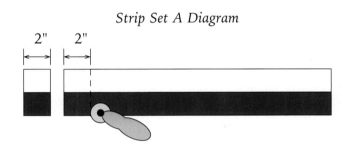

2. Join 2 segments as shown to make 1 Four-Patch A unit (*Unit A Assembly Diagrams*). Make 180 A units.

Unit A Assembly Diagrams

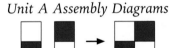

3. Join 1 white B and 1 pink C as shown in *Curve Unit Assembly Diagrams* to make 1 white curve unit. Press seams toward B. Make 72 white curve units. Repeat with pink Bs and white Cs to make 72 pink curve units. Press seams toward C.

Curve Unit Assembly Diagrams

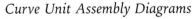
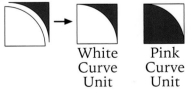

White Curve Unit   Pink Curve Unit

4. Lay out 5 A units, 2 pink curve units, and 2 white curve units as shown in *Block Assembly Diagram*. Join into rows; join rows to complete 1 Roller Coaster block. Make 36 identical Roller Coaster blocks.

Block Assembly Diagram

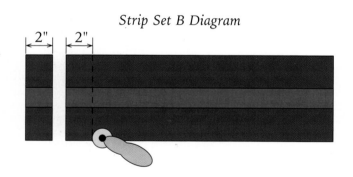

Quilt Assembly

1. Lay out blocks, carefully following *Quilt Top Assembly Diagram*, page 9. Join into rows; join rows to complete quilt center.
2. Join 2 (3" x 9") pink strips and 1 (2" x 9") black strip to make 1 strip set (*Strip Set B Diagram*). Cut strip set into 4 (2"-wide) center segments for border corners.

Strip Set B Diagram

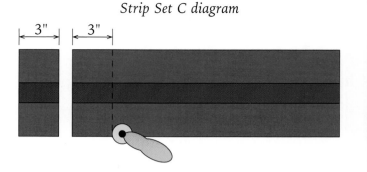

3. Join 2 (3" x 26") black strips and 1 (2" x 26") pink strip to make 1 strip set (*Strip Set C Diagram*). Cut strip set into 8 (3"-wide) side segments for border corners.

Strip Set C diagram

4. Join 2 C segments and 1 B segment as shown to make 1 border corner (*Border Corner Assembly Diagrams*). Repeat to make 4 border corners.

Border Corner Assembly Diagrams

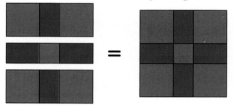

5. Join 2 (3"-wide) pink strips and 1 (2"-wide) black strip as shown in *Border Assembly Diagram* to make 1 border strip. Repeat to make 4 border strips.

Border Assembly Diagram

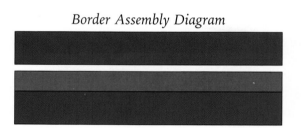

6. Referring to *Quilt Top Assembly Diagram*, join 1 border strip to side of quilt. Repeat for opposite side.
7. Join 1 border corner to each end of remaining border strips. Add strips to top and bottom of quilt.

Quilting and Finishing

1. Divide backing fabric into 2 (2-yard) lengths. Cut 1 piece in half lengthwise. Sew 1 narrow panel to each side of wide panel. Press seam allowances toward narrow panels.

2. Layer backing, batting, and quilt top; baste. Quilt as desired.

3. Join 2¼"-wide black strips into 1 continuous piece for straight-grain French-fold binding. Follow *Binding,* page 110, to add binding to quilt.

Quilt Top Assembly Diagram

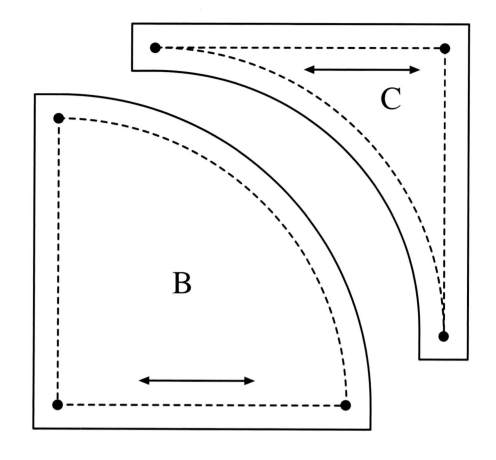

C

B

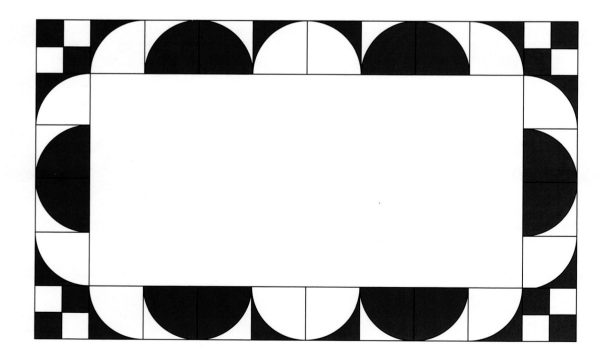

Trace, scan, or photocopy this quilt label to finish your quilt.
Leisure Arts, Inc., grants permission to photocopy this page for personal use only.

Conquer Curve-a-phobia

by Rhonda Richards

To tell the truth, curved seams are not nearly as difficult as I had imagined. In fact, curved piecing can actually be fun.

Let me share a few tricks I've learned. The main secrets for success are carefully pinning and gently tugging the fabric as you sew.

Normally, I piece without pinning, but that did not work well with curved seams. Then I went to the other extreme of pinning about every $1/4$". That didn't work either; I still got puckers when I pressed the block open. I found that five strategically placed silk pins work just fine. [Liz and Marianne find it easier to sew with the outer curved (convex) piece on top. However, I prefer to sew with the inner curved (concave) piece on the bottom. Experiment to see which method works best for you.]

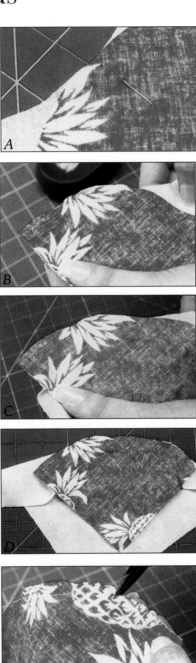

1. After you've cut out the curved pieces, fold each one in half and make a finger crease to find the center. With right sides facing, pin at the center match points (*photo A*.)

2. Next, align the raw edges of your inner and outer curved pieces along the left side and pin (*photo B*).

3. Aligning the curved edges, pin the loose area between the left side and the center (*photo C*).

4. Repeat Steps 2 and 3 for the right side of the curve. When you're done, the unit should look like *photo D*. The unit will look buckled, and you'll worry that this won't work. Stay calm: It will.

5. Now you're ready to sew. Go slowly. It is crucial to have a $1/4$" seam guide on your sewing machine to keep your seam even. Every few stitches pause to turn it and give the bottom piece a little tug. That will prevent puckers and tucks as you sew. However, you must take care to keep the raw edges of curves aligned.

6. Remove the pins. Make small clips along the curved seam allowance (*photo E*). This will make the curve lie flat.

7. Using a steam iron, press the seam allowance toward the darker fabric (*photo F*). You should have a beautiful curve with no tucks or puckers.

Flock of Birds

QUILT BY MARY RADKE

Finished Size: 42" x 42" (107 x 107 cm)
Blocks: 16 – 8" (20 cm) Bird Blocks

Dark reproduction prints combined with light plaids and shirting prints make a lovely decorative quilt look delightfully primitive. Pieced with a variety of fat quarters and fat eighths, this quaint accent is so simple you'll want to create several in an assortment of seasonal colors and prints.

Materials

8 fat eighths* assorted olive green and brown medium prints
8 fat quarters** blue and black dark prints
16 fat eighths* light prints
1/4 yard (23 cm) blue stripe for inner border
1/2 yard (46 cm) fabric for binding
2 2/3 yards (2.4 m) fabric for backing
Crib-size batting
*Fat eighth = 9" x 22" (23 x 56 cm)
**Fat quarter = 18" x 22" (46 x 56 cm)

Cutting

Measurements include 1/4" seam allowances. Cut crosswise strips unless otherwise noted. Follow *Rotary Cutting*, page 100.

From each medium fat eighth, cut:
- 2 (4 7/8") squares. Cut squares in half diagonally to make 32 half-square triangles (B).
- 5 (2 1/2" x 4 1/2") rectangles for border.

From each dark fat quarter, cut:
- 2 (4 7/8") squares. Cut squares in half diagonally to make 32 half-square triangles (B).
- 2 sets of 4 (2 7/8") squares. Cut squares in half diagonally to make 128 half-square triangles (A).
- 5 (2 1/2" x 4 1/2") rectangles for border.

From each light fat eighth, cut:
- 4 (2 7/8") squares. Cut squares in half diagonally to make 128 half-square triangles (A).
- 10 (2 1/2") squares for border. You will have a few extra.

From blue stripe, cut:
- 4 (1 1/2"-wide) strips for inner borders.

From binding fabric, cut:
- 5 (2 1/4"-wide) strips.

Block Assembly

1. Join light and dark As to make 128 triangle-square units. In quilt shown, light and dark triangles were combined in sets of 4 to 8 matching units, plus several non-matching units.
2. Referring to *Small Triangle Unit Assembly Diagram*, join 4 matching triangle-square units to make 1 small triangle Unit A. Make 32 small triangle units. In quilt shown, non-matching triangle squares were incorporated in several units.

Small Triangle Unit Assembly Diagram

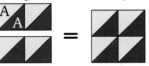

3. Join medium and dark Bs to make 32 Unit Bs. Quilt shown has 16 sets of 2 matching units.
4. Referring to *Block Assembly Diagram*, lay out 2 Unit As and 2 Unit Bs. Join to complete 1 block (*Block Diagram*).
5. Repeat to make 16 Bird blocks.

Block Assembly Diagram

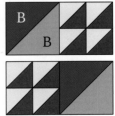

Block Diagram

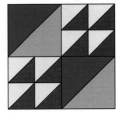

Quilt Assembly

1. Referring to *Quilt Top Assembly Diagram*, lay out blocks in 4 horizontal rows of 4 blocks each, positioning each block as shown. Join blocks into rows. Press seam allowances in opposite directions from row to row. Join rows.

2. Trim 2 blue stripe border strips to $32^1/_2$" long. Join to quilt top and bottom. Trim remaining 2 borders $34^1/_2$" long. Join to quilt sides.

3. Referring to *Goose Chase Unit Diagrams*, lay 1 ($2^1/_2$") light square atop 1 ($2^1/_2$" x $4^1/_2$") medium rectangle, with right sides facing, as shown in Step A.

Goose Chase Unit Diagrams

| Step A | Step B | Step C | Step D |

4. Stitch from corner to corner and trim $^1/_4$" away from seam as shown in Step B. Open out triangle as shown in Step C; press, pressing seam allowances toward small triangle.

5. Referring to Step C, lay 1 ($2^1/_2$") matching square atop remaining end of rectangle, with right sides facing. Stitch as shown and trim as before. Press seam allowance toward small triangle, as shown in Step D. Make 76 Goose Chase units, using medium and dark rectangles.

6. Join Goose Chase units to make 2 strips of 17 units and 2 strips of 21 units. Referring to *Quilt Top Assembly Diagram* for direction of units, join shorter strips to quilt top and bottom; then join longer strips to quilt sides. Press seam allowances toward inner border.

Quilting and Finishing

1. Divide backing fabric into 2 ($1^1/_3$-yard) lengths. From 1 length, cut 1 (7" x 48") strip. Join strip to lengthwise side of full-width piece. Press seam allowance in 1 direction.

2. Layer backing, batting, and quilt top; baste. Quilt as desired. Quilt shown was machine-quilted in-the-ditch along seam lines as shown in *Quilting Diagram*, page 15. Goose Chase border units were quilted in-the-ditch around large triangles.

3. Join $2^1/_4$"-wide strips into 1 continuous piece for straight-grain French-fold binding. Follow *Binding*, page 110, to add binding to quilt.

Quilt Top Assembly Diagram

Try This!

Pattern tester Pat Myers put an entirely new twist on this block by using Patricia Campbell and Michelle Jack's Fossil Fern collection by Benartex. The color scheme suggests that this Flock of Birds *may be heading back from the tropics!*

Lemon Zest

QUILT BY MARIANNE FONS; QUILTED BY LYNN WITZENBURG

Finished Size: 42" x 42" (107 x 107 cm)
Blocks: 9 – 10" (25 cm) Lemon Zest Blocks

Marianne created this light, summery quilt to show off her pretty blue and gold fabrics, but you can use fat quarters in your favorite hues, or even a holiday color scheme. If you're feeling a bit more wild or whimsical, choose a novelty print for the large block centers. Let the fabric inspire you to combine colors you normally might not try.

Materials

Fat quarter* light print #1 for Block As
Fat quarter* light print #2 for Block As
3/4 yard (69 cm) dark blue for border, binding, and leaves in Block Bs
1/2 yard (46 cm) light blue for leaves in Block Bs
1/2 yard (46 cm) medium blue floral for Block B centers and border corners
Fat quarter* yellow #1 for Block B background
1/2 yard (46 cm) yellow #2 for Block B background
Fat quarter* yellow #3 for Block A leaves
Fat quarter* yellow-and-blue floral for Block As
3/4 yard (69 cm) yellow-and-blue plaid for Block A leaves and border
1 1/4 yards (1.1 m) backing
Crib-size batting
Template material
*Fat quarter = 18" x 22"

Cutting

Measurements include 1/4" seam allowances. Border strips are exact length needed. You may want to cut them longer to allow for piecing variations. Cut crosswise strips unless otherwise noted. Follow *Rotary Cutting,* page 100. Make template for pattern D on page 18.

From light print #1, cut:
• 3 (3"-wide) strips. Cut strips into 16 (3") squares (C) for Block As.

From light print #2, cut:
• 5 (3"-wide) strips. Cut strips into 16 (3" x 5 1/2") rectangles (B) for Block As.

From dark blue, cut:
• 4 (1 1/2"-wide) strips. Cut strips into 2 (1 1/2" x 30 1/2") side borders and 2 (1 1/2" x 32 1/2") top and bottom borders.
• 20 leaves D.
• 5 (2 1/4"-wide) strips for binding.

From light blue, cut:
• 40 leaves D.
From medium blue floral, cut:
• 2 (5 1/2"-wide) strips. Cut strips into 9 (5 1/2") squares (A) for Block B centers and border corners.
From yellow #1, cut:
• 3 (3"-wide) strips. Cut strips into 20 (3") squares (C) for Block Bs.
From yellow #2, cut:
• 5 (3"-wide) strips. Cut strips into 20 (3" x 5 1/2") rectangles (B) for Block Bs.
From yellow #3, cut:
• 32 leaves D.
From yellow-and-blue floral, cut:
• 2 (5 1/2"-wide) strips. Cut strips into 4 (5 1/2") squares (A) for Block As.
From yellow-and-blue plaid, cut:
• 4 (5 1/2"-wide) strips. Cut strips into 4 (5 1/2" x 32 1/2") outer borders.
• 16 leaves D.

Block A Assembly

1. To make 1 Block A, join 1 light #2 B rectangle to each side of 1 yellow-and-blue floral A square, as shown in *Block A Assembly Diagram.*
2. Join 1 light #1 C square to each end of 1 light #2 B rectangle. Repeat. Join to top and bottom of previous A/B unit.
3. Appliqué 4 yellow-and-blue plaid Ds and 8 yellow #3 Ds in place as shown to complete 1 Block A (*Block A Diagram*).
4. Make 4 Block As.

Block A Assembly Diagram

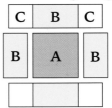

Block A Diagram

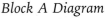
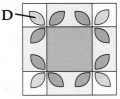

Block B Assembly

1. To make 1 Block B, join 1 yellow #2 B rectangle to each side of 1 medium blue floral A square, as shown in *Block B Assembly Diagram*.
2. Join 1 yellow #1 C square to each end of 1 yellow #2 B rectangle. Repeat. Join to top and bottom of previous A/B unit.
3. Appliqué 4 dark blue Ds and 8 light blue Ds in place to complete 1 Block B (*Block B Diagram*).
4. Make 5 Block Bs.

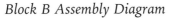

Block B Assembly Diagram   *Block B Diagram*

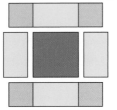 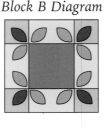

Quilt Assembly

1. Lay out blocks as shown in *Quilt Top Assembly Diagram*, page 19. Join into rows; join rows to complete center.
2. Add blue side borders to opposite sides of quilt top. Press seam allowance toward borders. Add remaining 2 blue borders to top and bottom of quilt.
3. Join 1 yellow check border to each side of quilt. Add 1 medium blue floral square to ends of remaining border strips. Add to top and bottom of quilt.

Quilting and Finishing

1. Layer backing, batting, and quilt top; baste. Quilt as desired. Quilt shown was quilted in-the-ditch around blocks, appliqué, and blue border. Squares have a diagonal grid, and outer border features a braid pattern.
2. Join 2$\frac{1}{4}$"-wide dark blue strips into 1 continuous strip to make straight-grain French-fold binding. Follow *Binding*, page 110, to add binding to quilt.

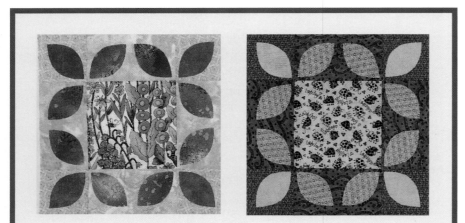

The large block center of Lemon Zest *offers a great opportunity to show off novelty prints. In these examples, Laura Morris Edwards used colorful bug prints to create a whimsical, summery look. When you begin with a wild novelty print, you may find yourself combining colors you normally wouldn't try.*

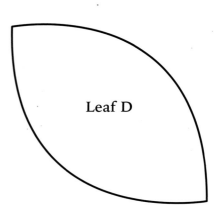

Pattern shown is finished size. Add
$\frac{3}{16}$" seam allowance for hand appliqué
or cut finished size for fusing.

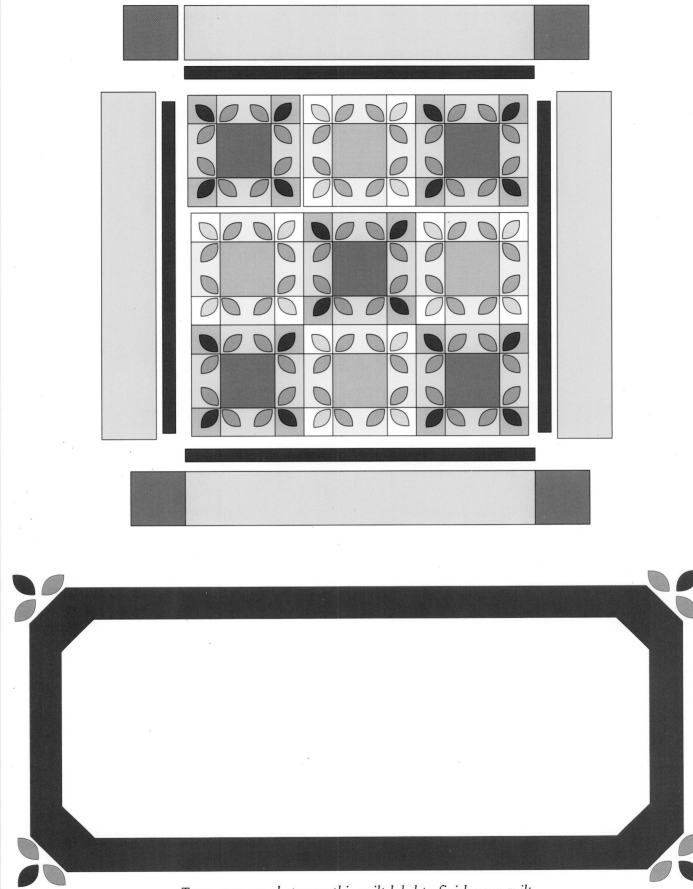

Trace, scan, or photocopy this quilt label to finish your quilt.
Leisure Arts, Inc., grants permission to photocopy this page for personal use only.

Welcome Home Table Runner

DESIGNED AND MADE BY JOLYN M. OLSON

Finished Size: 15" x 35" (38 x 89 cm)
Blocks: 3 – 5" (13 cm) Variable Star Blocks
and 2 – 5" (13 cm) House Blocks

Use your scraps to make this old-fashioned table runner in a jiffy. Variable Star and House blocks combine with a Goose Chase border to make this folksy runner oh-so charming. When you're ready to display your new creation, think outside the dining room; table runners make welcoming accents in the den, living room, or bedroom — anyplace you have a table!

Materials

$^1/_2$ yard (46 cm) total assorted light print scraps, at least 2" (5 cm) square, for blocks

$^1/_2$ yard (46 cm) total medium/dark print scraps, at least 2" x 3" (5 x 8 cm), for blocks (Project shown uses red, blue, green, brown, gold, and black.)

$^1/_8$ yard (11 cm) or scraps 2 different light check prints for House blocks

$^1/_8$ yard (11 cm) or scrap solid black for House blocks

$^1/_2$ yard (46 cm) blue print for borders and binding

$^1/_2$ yard (46 cm) blue paisley for backing

Batting scrap at least 20" x 40" (51 x 102 cm)

Variable Star Blocks Cutting

Measurements include $^1/_4$" seam allowances. Borders are exact length needed.

From 3 different light prints, cut 1 set from each:
- 4 ($1^3/_4$") squares for background.
- 4 ($1^3/_4$" x 3") rectangles for background.

From 3 different dark prints, cut 1 set from each:
- 8 ($1^3/_4$") squares for star points.

From 1 red, blue, and green dark prints, cut 1 from each:
- 1 (3") square for star center.

Variable Star Block Assembly

1. Using diagonal-corners method, position 1 ($1^3/_4$") dark square on 1 ($1^3/_4$" x 3") light rectangle, right sides facing, aligning corners as shown in *Diagonal Corners Diagrams*. Sew across diagonal of square. Trim excess fabric $^1/_4$" from seam. Press open. Repeat on opposite end with matching dark square to make 1 Goose Chase unit for star points. Make 4 matching units.

Diagonal Corners Diagrams

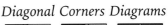

2. Lay out 4 matching light $1^3/_4$" squares, 4 completed star point units from Step 1, and 1 (3") center square as shown in *Variable Star Block Assembly Diagram*. Join into rows; join rows to complete block.

3. Repeat to make 3 Variable Star blocks (*Variable Star Block Diagram*).

Variable Star Block Assembly Diagram

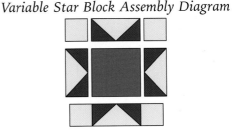

Variable Star Block Diagram

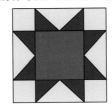

House Blocks Cutting

From 1 blue and 1 red dark print, cut 1 from each:
- 1 ($1^1/2$" x $5^1/2$") rectangle for roof.

From black, cut:
- 6 ($1^1/2$") squares for windows and chimneys.
- 2 ($1^1/2$" x $2^1/2$") rectangles for doors.

From 2 different light prints, cut 1 set from each:
- 5 ($1^1/2$") squares for sky.

From 2 different checks, cut 1 from each:
- 1 ($1^1/2$" x $5^1/2$") rectangle for top of house.
- 1 ($1^1/2$" x $2^1/2$") rectangle for side of door.
- 1 ($1^1/2$" x $3^1/2$") rectangle for below window.
- 2 ($1^1/2$") squares for sides of window.

House Block Assembly

1. Referring to *House Block Assembly Diagram*, join 3 ($1^1/2$") light squares and 2 ($1^1/2$") black squares alternately to make chimney unit.
2. Using diagonal-seams method, join 1 ($1^1/2$") light square to each end of red and blue $1^1/2$" x $5^1/2$" rectangles to make roof unit.
3. Join 1 ($1^1/2$" x $2^1/2$") check rectangle and 1 ($1^1/2$" x $2^1/2$") black rectangle on long sides to make door unit.
4. Join 2 ($1^1/2$") check squares and 1 ($1^1/2$") black square alternately to make window unit. Join to 1 ($1^1/2$" x $3^1/2$") check rectangle.
5. Lay out chimney unit, roof unit, 1 ($1^1/2$" x $5^1/2$", page 21) check rectangle, door unit, and window unit as shown. Join door and window units. Join rows to complete block.
6. Repeat to make 2 House blocks (*House Block Diagram*).

House Block Assembly Diagram   *House Block Diagram*

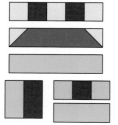
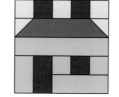

Goose Chase Border Cutting

From assorted light prints, cut:
- 128 ($1^3/4$") squares in sets of 2 for background.

From assorted medium/dark prints, cut:
- 64 ($1^3/4$" x 3") rectangles for unit centers.

From 4 different brown prints, cut:
- 1 (3") square from each.

From blue print, cut:
- 5 ($1^3/4$"-wide) strips. Cut strips into:
  - 2 ($1^3/4$" x 28") strips for outer side borders.
  - 2 ($1^3/4$" x $25^1/2$") strips for inner side borders.
  - 4 ($1^3/4$" x 8") strips for top and bottom borders.
  - 4 ($1^3/4$") squares for border corners.

Goose Chase Border Assembly

1. Referring to *Diagonal Corners Diagrams*, page 21, position 1 ($1^3/4$") light square on 1 ($1^3/4$" x 3") medium/dark rectangle. Stitch across diagonal of square, trim, and press. Repeat on opposite end with matching light square to make 1 Goose Chase unit.
2. Repeat to make 64 Goose Chase units.
3. Join 11 Goose Chase units, pointing in same direction, into a strip. Make 4 strips. Join ends of 2 strips with points facing to make 1 side border (*Table Runner Top Assembly Diagram*, page 23). Repeat to make second border.
4. Join 3 Goose Chase units, pointing in the same direction, into a strip. Make 4 strips. Join ends of 2 strips with points facing to make 1 end border. Repeat to make second border.
5. Join 1 (3") brown square to each end of short Goose Chase borders. Add 1 Goose Chase unit to each end of these border strips, pointing out.
6. Join 2 ($1^3/4$") blue squares, 2 Goose Chase units, and 1 ($1^3/4$" x 8") blue strip end to end as shown in *Table Runner Top Assembly Diagram*. Press seam allowances toward blue strips and squares. Make 2 strips. Add 1 strip each to top and bottom border.

Table Runner Assembly

1. Join Variable Star blocks and House blocks into a strip as shown in *Table Runner Top Assembly Diagram.*
2. Add 1 ($1^3/_4$" x $25^1/_2$") blue strip to each side. Press seam allowances toward border strips. Add 1 ($1^3/_4$" x 8") blue strip to top and bottom.
3. Add 1 (22-unit) Goose Chase strip to each side. Add 1 ($1^3/_4$" x 28") blue strip to each side.
4. Add top and bottom borders, aligning seams.

Quilting and Finishing

1. Layer backing, batting, and quilt top; baste. Quilt as desired. Quilt shown was machine quilted in-the-ditch.
2. For binding, cut 3 ($2^1/_4$"-wide) strips from blue print. Make approximately 3 yards of straight-grain French-fold binding. Follow *Binding*, page 110, to add binding to quilt.

Table Runner Top Assembly Diagram

23

Liberty Rose

QUILT BY KATIE PORTER; QUILTED BY LYNN WITZENBURG

Finished Size: 76" x 106¹/₂" (193 x 271 cm)
Blocks: 8 – 20" (51 cm) Liberty Rose Blocks

An antique quilt in a book about Nebraska quiltmakers inspired *Liberty Rose*. Katie Porter, Liz's daughter, used modern techniques — such as fusing with web, machine appliquéing, and machine quilting — to make her contemporary version.

Materials

7 yards (6.4 m) light print for background
3¼ yards (3 m) red print #1 for sashing, borders, and binding
1 yard (91 cm) navy print for appliqué
¾ yard (69 cm) gold check for appliqué
1¾ yards (1.6 m) green print for vines and leaves
½ yard (46 cm) red print #2 for appliqué
6½ yards (5.9 m) fabric for backing
Queen-size batting
Template material

Cutting

Measurements include ¼" seam allowances. Cut crosswise strips unless otherwise noted. Follow *Rotary Cutting*, page 100. Appliqué patterns are on page 28.
From light print, cut:
- 3 yards. Cut into 8 (2"-wide) lengthwise strips. Cut strips into 4 (2" x 108") side borders and 4 (2" x 80") top and bottom borders.
  - From remainder, cut 5 (20½") squares for block backgrounds.
- 2 (20½"-wide) strips. Cut strips into 3 (20½") squares, for a total of 8 block backgrounds.
- 2 (30"-wide) strips. Cut strips into 2 (30") squares. Cut squares in quarters diagonally to make 8 side setting triangles. You will have 2 extra.
- 1 (15¼"-wide) strip. Cut strip into 2 (15¼") squares. Cut squares in half diagonally to make 4 corner triangles.
From red print #1, cut:
- 17 (2"-wide) lengthwise strips. Cut strips into:
- 6 (2" x 108") side borders.
- 6 (2" x 80") top and bottom borders.
- 2 (2" x 66½") medium sashing strips.
- 1 (2" x 88") long center sashing strip.
- 12 (2" x 20½") sashing strips.
- 2 (2" x 23½") outside sashing strips.

- 4 (2¼"-wide) lengthwise strips for binding.
From navy print, cut:
- 62 stars (E).
From gold check, cut:
- 8 wreaths (D).
- 52 flower centers (B).
From green print, cut:
- 134 leaves (C).
- 1⅛"-wide bias strips. Fold lengthwise into thirds and press. Cut bias into:
  - 32 (6½"-long) pieces for block vines.
  - 6 (12½"-long) pieces for side setting triangles.
  - 8 (5½"-long) pieces for corner triangle vines.
From red print #2, cut:
- 52 flowers (A).

Block Assembly

1. Fold 1 (20½") square in quarters and in halves to make crease lines for appliqué placement. Referring to *Block Diagram*, appliqué the following: 4 block vines, 4 flowers (A), 4 flower centers (B), 12 leaves (C), 1 wreath (D), and 5 stars (E).
2. Make 8 Liberty Rose blocks.

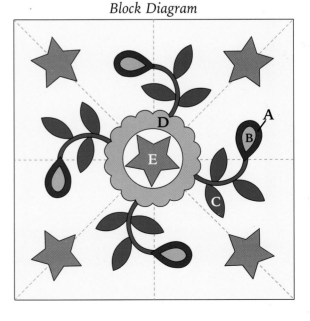

Block Diagram

3. Referring to *Side Setting Triangle Diagram,* appliqué the following: 1 setting triangle vine, 2 flowers (A), 2 flower centers (B), 5 leaves (C), and 3 stars (E).
4. Make 6 side setting triangles.

Side Setting Triangle Diagram

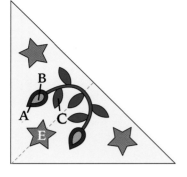

5. Referring to *Corner Triangle Diagram,* appliqué the following: 1 vine, 2 flowers (A), 2 flower centers (B), 2 leaves (C), and 1 star (E).
6. Make 4 corner triangles.

Corner Triangle Diagram

Quilt Assembly

1. Lay out blocks, setting triangles, and sashing strips as shown in *Quilt Top Assembly Diagram,* page 27. Join into diagonal rows; join with long sashing strips to complete center.
2. Using a long ruler, trim sashing ends even with setting triangles.
3. Join 3 red and 2 white border strips as shown. Repeat to make 4 border sets. Center and stitch border sets to quilt, beginning and ending seams exactly $1/4$" from each corner of quilt top. Backstitch at beginning and ending of stitching to reinforce. Fold one corner of quilt top diagonally with right sides together and matching edges. Use ruler to mark stitching line as shown in *Mitered Corner Diagram.* Sew on drawn line, backstitching at beginning and ending of stitching. Trim seam allowance to $1/4$" and press to one side. Repeat for other corners.

Mitered Corner Diagram

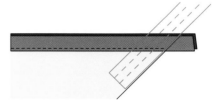

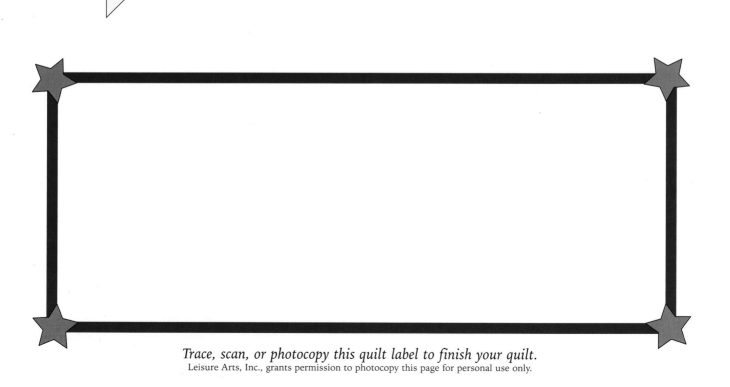

Trace, scan, or photocopy this quilt label to finish your quilt.

Quilting and Finishing

1. Divide backing fabric into 2 (3¼-yard) lengths. Cut 1 piece in half lengthwise. Sew 1 narrow panel to each side of wide panel. Press seam allowances toward narrow panels.

2. Layer backing, batting, and quilt top; baste. Quilt as desired. Quilt shown was outline-quilted around appliqué, and block background was filled with 1" grid. Red sashing features a wave pattern, and outer border sets have a star and swag design.

3. Join 2¼"-wide red strips for binding into 1 continuous strip to make straight-grain French-fold binding. Follow *Binding*, page 110, to add binding to quilt.

Quilt Top Assembly Diagram

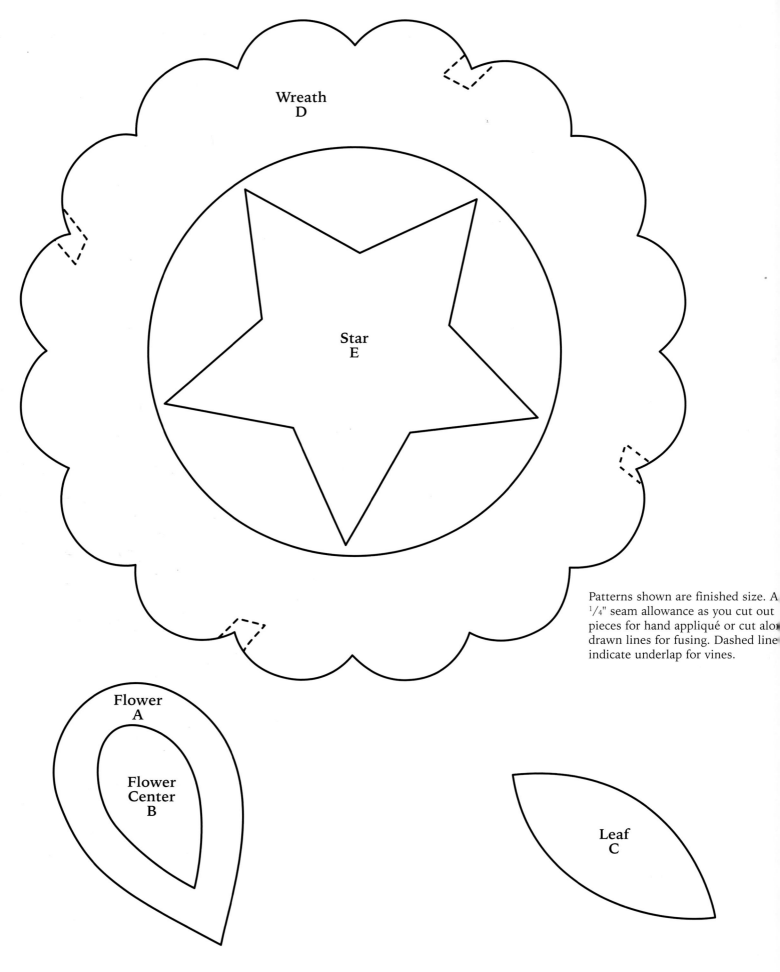

Wreath
D

Star
E

Patterns shown are finished size. A $^1/_4$" seam allowance as you cut out pieces for hand appliqué or cut alo drawn lines for fusing. Dashed line indicate underlap for vines.

Flower
A

Flower
Center
B

Leaf
C

Using Triangle Rulers

Triangle rulers, designed for cutting right triangles with legs on the straight-of-grain, let you cut triangles and squares of the same finished size from a single strip.

With most cutting tools, you need one size strip to cut squares and another size to cut triangles even if the edges of the squares and triangles have the same *finished* size. Extra fabric at the triangle tips creates the discrepancy in cut size.

Those tips get trimmed from the seam allowance in the end, so by eliminating this extra fabric from the start, you can cut both shapes from the same strip.

Triangle rulers, designed for cutting right triangles with legs on the straight-of-grain, let you cut triangles and squares of the same finished size from one strip. These rulers are available in several sizes and configurations. For this application, choose a ruler that measures the length of the triangle leg.

The strips below illustrate how to use a triangle ruler.

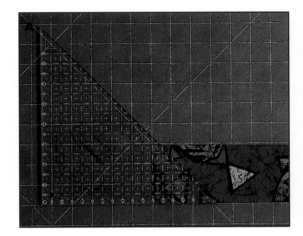

1. Cut fabric strip $1/2$" wider than desired *finished* size of squares or triangle legs. For our example, we cut $2^{1}/_2$"-wide strip that will give us 2" finished squares and triangles with 2" finished legs. Square off left end of strip.

2. Align bottom of ruler with bottom of strip *(photo A)*. Slide ruler to left until markings on ruler are correctly aligned for size you want to cut ($2^{1}/_2$" in our example).

3. Cut along slanted edge of ruler *(photo B)*. Top tip of cut triangle will be blunt because there is no excess fabric beyond seam allowance.

4. To cut next triangle, reposition ruler as shown *(photo C)*, aligning diagonal edge of ruler with cut edge of fabric. Cut along straight side of ruler. Continue alternating position of ruler to cut additional triangles.

Snailville

QUILT BY SUZANNE MARSHALL

Finished Size: 74¹/₂" x 98¹/₂" (189 x 250 cm)
Blocks: 18 – 12" (30 cm) House Blocks, and
17 – 12" (30 cm) Tree Blocks

"When I started making *Snailville*, I was looking for a 'quickie' patchwork pattern," says Suzanne Marshall, "but I wanted a different setting for the houses. Since I like to mix patchwork with appliqué, I added trees. When I finished the squares, I felt they needed perking up, so I added snails to the trees in different places. It's fun to look for the snail on each tree!"

Materials

¼ yard (23 cm) total [or 18 – 2" x 11"
    (5 x 28 cm) scraps] assorted gold prints
    for windows and snail shells
1¼ yards (1.1 m) total [or 18 – 5" x 15"
    (13 x 38 cm) scraps] assorted dark gold
    and brown prints for doors and roofs
½ yard (46 cm) total [or 18 – 4" x 10"
    (10 x 25 cm) scraps] assorted medium
    teals and blues for house fronts
⅞ yard (80 cm) total [or 18 – 1½"-wide
    (4 cm) strips] assorted dark teals and
    blues for house fronts and snail bodies
¼ yard (23 cm) green for lawn
⅛ yard (11 cm) gold grid print for sidewalk
⅛ yard (11 cm) gold brick print for chimneys
½ yard (46 cm) brown-and-gold swirl print
    for gables
½ yard (46 cm) gold-and-brown cobblestone
    print for block corner squares
3½ yards (3.2 m) blue mottle print for block
    background
1¾ yards (1.6 m) brown print for tree trucks
2 yards (1.8 m) total assorted green prints (at
    least 10) for tree leaves
½ yard (46 cm) dark gold for inner border
    [3 yards (2.7 m) for unpieced borders]
3 yards (2.7 m) blue print for outer border
    and binding
Brown embroidery floss
6 yards (5.5 m) fabric for backing
Queen-size batting

Cutting

Measurements include ¼" seam allowances. Cut crosswise strips unless otherwise noted. Follow *Rotary Cutting*, page 100. Patterns are on pages 34 and 35.

From assorted gold prints, cut:
- 17 snail shells (V).
- 18 sets of 2 (1½") squares (A) and 2 (1½" x 2½") rectangles (B) for windows.

From assorted dark gold and brown prints, cut:
- 18 sets of 1 H and 1 H reversed for roof.
- 18 (2½" x 4½") assorted rectangles (F) for doors.

From assorted medium teals and blues, cut:
- 18 sets of 1 (2½") square (E, above door) and 2 (1½" x 6½") rectangles (D, door sides).

From assorted dark teals and blues, cut:
- 17 snail bodies (U).
- 18 sets of 6 (1½") squares (A) and 4 (1½" x 6½") rectangles (D) for window backgrounds.

From green, cut:
- 5 (1½"-wide) strips. Cut strips into 18 (1½" x 5½") rectangles (K) and 18 (1½" x 4½") rectangles (L) for lawn.

From gold grid print, cut:
- 2 (1½"-wide) strips. Cut strips into 18 (1½" x 3½") rectangles (J) for sidewalk.

From gold brick print, cut:
- 1 (1½"-wide) strip. Cut strip into 18 (1½") squares (A) for chimneys.

From brown-and-gold swirl print, cut:
- 18 gables (G).

From gold-and-brown cobblestone print, cut:
- 3 (1½"-wide) strips. Cut strips into 68 (1½") squares (R) for tree block outer corner squares.
- 4 (2"-wide) strips. Cut strips into 68 (2") squares (P) for tree block inner corner squares.

From blue mottle print, cut:

- 36 (1½"-wide) strips. Cut strips into:
  - 18 each of I and I reversed for house block.
  - 18 (1½" x 2½") rectangles (B) for house block.
  - 18 (1½" x 7½") rectangles (C) for house block.
  - 36 (1½" x 12½") rectangles (M) for house block.
  - 68 (1½" x 10½") rectangles (Q) for tree block.
- 7 (7½"-wide) strips. Cut strips into 17 (7½") squares (N) and 68 (2" x 7½") rectangles (O) for tree blocks.

From brown print, cut:
- 17 free-form tree trunks (S), or use pattern on page 34.

From assorted green prints, cut:
- 136 to 170 free-form leaf clusters (T) or use pattern on page 34.

From dark gold, cut:
- 10 (1¼"-wide) strips. Piece to make 4 (1¼" x 100") inner border strips. If you prefer unpieced borders, cut 4 (1¼"-wide) lengthwise strips from alternate yardage.

From blue print, cut:
- 4 (7"-wide) lengthwise strips for outer border.
- 4 (2¼"-wide) lengthwise strips for binding.

House Block Assembly

Refer to *House Block Assembly Diagram* throughout.
1. Join 1 blue C, 1 chimney A, and 1 blue B as shown to make Row 1.
2. Join 1 blue I, 1 roof H, 1 gable G, 1 roof H reversed, and 1 blue I reversed as shown to make Row 2.
3. Join 1 gold window A, 1 gold window B, and 3 window background As into a strip as shown in Row 3. Join 1 window background D strip to each side to make 1 window unit. Repeat to make 2 matching window units.
4. Join 1 door F and 1 door background E as shown. Join 1 door background D to each side to make 1 door unit. Join 1 window unit to each side of door unit to complete Row 3.
5. Referring to *Diagonal Seams Diagrams,* join 1

sidewalk J to 1 lawn K as shown. Join 1 lawn L to opposite end of J to complete Row 4.

Diagonal Seams Diagrams.

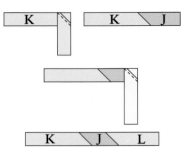

6. Join Rows 1 through 4. Add 1 blue M to each side to complete 1 House block (*House Block Diagram*).
7. Make 18 House blocks.

House Block Assembly Diagram

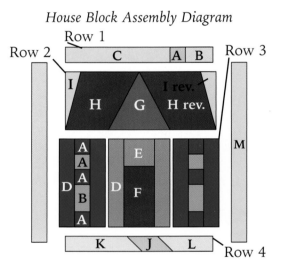

House Block Diagram

32

Tree Block Assembly

Refer to *Tree Block Assembly Diagram* throughout.

1. Join 1 blue O strip to each side of 1 blue N square. Add P squares to each end of remaining O strips. Add to top and bottom of block.
2. Join 1 blue Q strip to each side of block. Add R squares to each end of remaining Q strips. Add to top and bottom of block to complete block background.

Tree Block Assembly Diagram

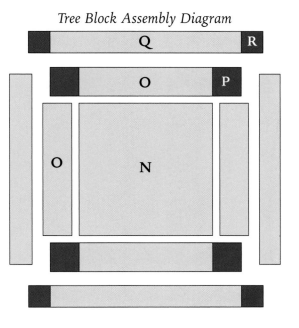

3. Use *Tree Block Diagram* as guide for appliqué. Appliqué in following order, using any appliqué technique desired: 1 tree trunk (S), 8 to 10 leaf clusters (T), 1 snail body (U), and 1 snail shell (V). Embroider shell detail, eye, and antennae with brown embroidery floss.
4. Make 17 Tree blocks.

Tree Block Diagram

Quilt Assembly

1. Alternate 3 House blocks and 2 Tree blocks. Join blocks to make 1 horizontal House row. Make 4 House rows.
2. Alternate 3 Tree blocks and 2 House blocks. Join blocks to make 1 horizontal Tree row. Make 3 Tree rows.
3. Alternate House rows and Tree rows. Join rows to complete center.
4. Join 1 gold border strip to 1 blue border strip along length to make border strip set. Make 4 border strip sets. Center and stitch border sets to quilt, beginning and ending seams exactly 1/4" from each corner of quilt top. Backstitch at beginning and ending of stitching to reinforce. Fold one corner of quilt top diagonally with right sides together and matching edges. Use ruler to mark stitching line as shown in *Mitered Corner Diagram*. Sew on drawn line, backstitching at beginning and ending of stitching. Trim seam allowance to 1/4" and press to one side. Repeat for other corners.

Mitered Corner Diagram

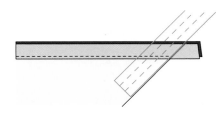

Quilting and Finishing

1. Divide backing fabric into 2 (3-yard) lengths. Cut 1 piece in half lengthwise. Sew 1 narrow panel to each side of wide panel. Press seam allowances toward narrow panels.
2. Layer backing, batting, and quilt top; baste. Quilt as desired. Quilt shown was outline-quilted in House blocks, with vertical waves in D sections and diamonds quilted into doors and E pieces. Tree blocks were quilted around appliqué, with diagonals filling background. Border features a Celtic knot design.
3. Join 2 1/4"-wide blue strips for binding into 1 continuous strip to make straight-grain French-fold binding. Follow *Binding*, page 110, to add binding to quilt.

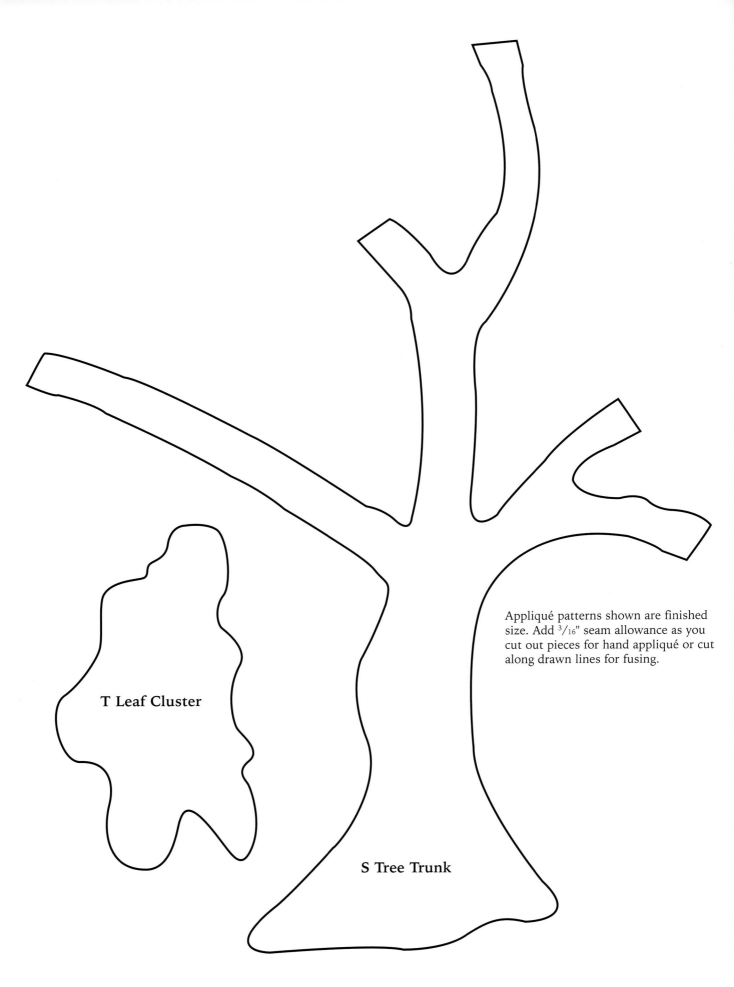

T Leaf Cluster

Appliqué patterns shown are finished
size. Add ³/₁₆" seam allowance as you
cut out pieces for hand appliqué or cut
along drawn lines for fusing.

S Tree Trunk

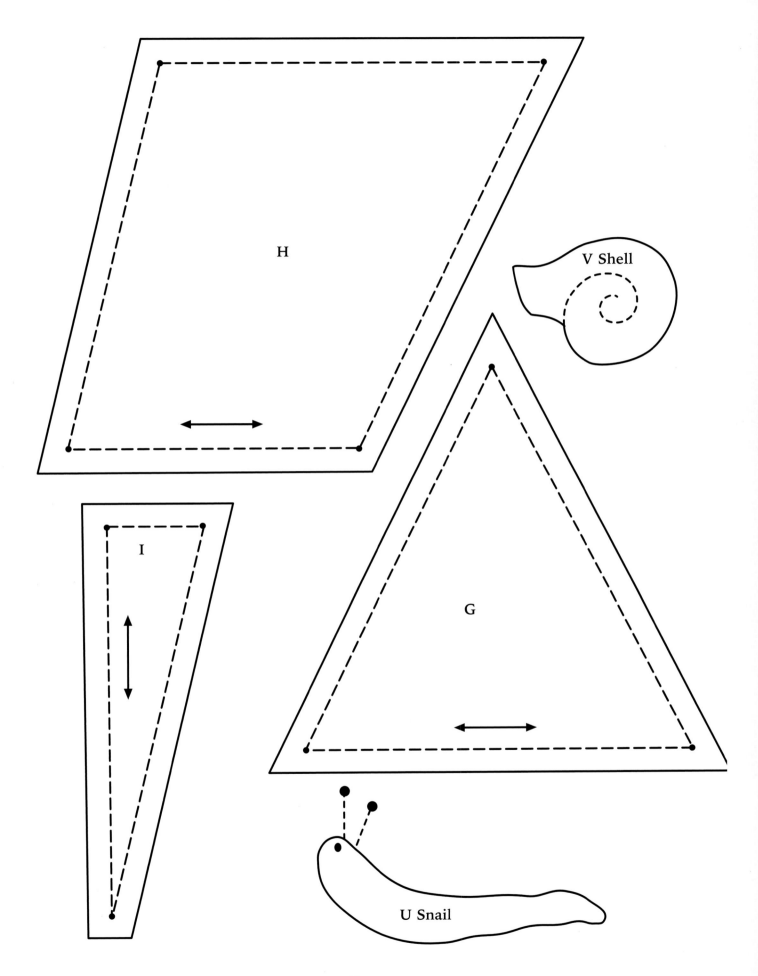

H

V Shell

I

G

U Snail

Spring Mountain Rose

QUILT BY CHARLOTTE HUBER; INSPIRED BY *SPRING WREATH* IN
MOUNTAIN MIST QUILT FAVORITES (WWW.STEARNSTEXTILES.COM)

Finished Size: 75" x 75" (191 x 191 cm)
Blocks: 36 – 7¹/₂" (19 cm) Delectable Mountains Blocks

The mountains are alive with the scent of flowers and the colors of spring. A trip to the Great Smoky Mountains inspired Charlotte Huber to make *Spring Mountain Rose*. She chose the traditional Delectable Mountains block, stitching it in springtime green. The quilt won honorable mention at the Smoky Mountain Quilt Show in Knoxville, Tennessee.

Materials

$2^3/4$ yards (2.5 m) green print for blocks and binding
6 yards (5.5 m) white-on-white print for blocks and border
$3/4$ yard (69 cm) pink print for posies and tulip tips
$1/4$ yard (23 cm) red print for tulips and posy centers
1 yard (91 cm) dark green print for stems and leaves
$4^1/2$ yards (4.1 m) backing
Full-size batting

Cutting

Measurements include $1/4$" seam allowances. Setting triangles are oversize to allow for trimming. Cut crosswise strips unless otherwise noted. Follow *Rotary Cutting*, page 100. Patterns are on page 42.
From green print, cut:
• 8 ($2^1/4$"-wide) strips for binding.
• 20 ($2^3/8$"-wide) strips. Cut strips into 312 ($2^3/8$") squares. Cut squares in half diagonally to make 624 A triangles for blocks and borders.
• 3 ($6^7/8$"-wide) strips. Cut strips into 18 ($6^7/8$") squares. Cut squares in half diagonally to make 36 C triangles for blocks.

From white-on-white print, cut:
• $2^1/4$ yards. Cut yardage into 4 (8"-wide) lengthwise strips for appliqué border.
• 1 ($15^1/2$") square for center block.
• 20 ($2^3/8$"-wide) strips. Cut strips into 312 ($2^3/8$") squares. Cut squares in half diagonally to make 624 A triangles for blocks and borders.
• 3 (2"-wide) strips. Cut strips into 44 (2") B squares.
• 3 ($6^7/8$"-wide) strips. Cut strips into 18 ($6^7/8$") squares. Cut squares in half diagonally to make 36 C triangles for blocks.
• 2 (13"-wide) strips. Cut strips into 5 (13") squares. Cut squares in quarters diagonally to make 20 D setting triangles.
From pink print, cut:
• 20 small posies (F).
• 32 large posies (G).
• 32 tulip centers (H).
From red print, cut:
• 32 tulips (I).
• 52 posy centers (H).
From dark green print, cut:
• 400" of $3/4$"-wide bias. Fold lengthwise into thirds and press to make bias for stems. Cut 68 (5"-long) pieces for long stems and 16 (3"-long) pieces for short stems.
• 288 leaves (E).

Block Assembly

1. Join 1 green and 1 white A triangle to make 1 A unit (*A Unit Diagram*). Make 8 A units.

A Unit Diagram

2. Join 1 green and 1 white C triangle to make 1 C unit.
3. Referring to *Block Assembly Diagram*, join 4 A units. Join to 1 side of C unit.
4. Join 4 A units and 1 B square as shown. Join to top of C unit as shown to complete 1 Delectable Mountains block (*Block Diagram*).
5. Make 36 Delectable Mountains blocks.

Block Assembly Diagram

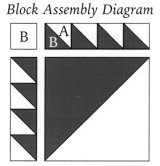

Block Diagram

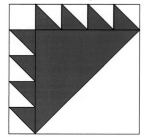

Border Assembly

1. Join 1 green and 1 white A triangle to make 1 A unit. Make 336 A units.
2. Join 36 A units into 1 strip, reversing direction at center of strip as shown in *Quilt Top Assembly Diagram* on page 41 to make 1 inner border. Repeat to make 4 inner borders.
3. Repeat step 2 with 48 A units in each strip for outer borders.

Center Block Assembly

1. Fold and crease center block to form guidelines for appliqué.
2. Referring to *Center Appliqué Diagram*, appliqué in order: 8 long stems, 32 E leaves, 4 G large posies, 4 H posy centers, 4 H tulip tips, and 4 I tulips.

Center Appliqué Diagram

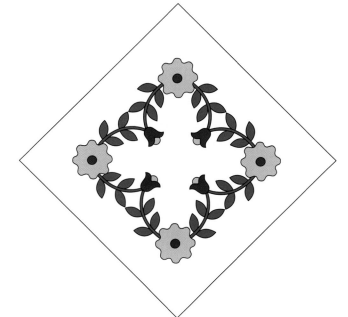

Setting Triangle Assembly

1. Join 2 D triangles as shown in *Corner 1 Appliqué Diagram*. Appliqué in order: 2 short stems, 1 long stem, 6 E leaves, 3 F small posies, and 3 H posy centers to complete 1 corner setting triangle block.
2. Repeat to make 4 corner setting triangle blocks.

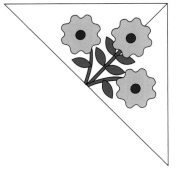

Corner 1 Appliqué Diagram

Quilt Assembly

1. Lay out blocks and setting triangles as shown in *Quilt Top Assembly Diagram*, page 41. Join into sections as shown, aligning outer triangles so that excess is to be outside of quilt.
2. Before joining sections, appliqué 4 two-block units *(Corner 2 Appliqué Diagram)* that touch center block. Appliqué in order: 2 short stems, 2 E leaves, 2 F small posies, and 2 H posy centers in each area.

Corner 2 Appliqué Diagram

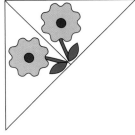

3. Join sections to complete inner quilt. Trim inner quilt evenly to 54$\frac{1}{2}$" square. This is to ensure that inner border will fit.
4. Join 1 (36-unit) inner border strip to opposite sides of center section. Add 1 B square to each end of remaining inner border strips and add to quilt.
5. Center and stitch 8" wide strip to each side of quilt, beginning and ending seams exactly $\frac{1}{4}$" from each corner of quilt top. Backstitch at beginning and ending of stitching to reinforce. Fold one corner of quilt top diagonally with right sides together and matching edges. Use ruler to mark stitching line as shown in *Mitered Corner Diagram*. Sew on drawn line, backstitching at beginning and ending of stitching. Trim seam allowance to $\frac{1}{4}$" and press to one side. Repeat for other corners. Quilt should measure 72$\frac{1}{2}$" square. Trim to size if needed so outer borders will fit.

Mitered Corner Diagram

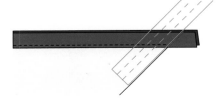

6. Join 1 (48-unit) outer border strip to opposite sides of quilt. Add 1 B square to each end of remaining outer border strips and add to quilt.

7. Appliqué outer border, spacing elements evenly. Appliqué in order on each side: 14 long stems, 56 E leaves, 6 G large posies, 6 H posy centers, 7 H tulip tips, and 7 I tulips. In each corner, appliqué 1 G large posy and 1 H posy center as shown in *Border Appliqué Diagram* to complete quilt.

Quilting and Finishing

1. Divide backing fabric into 2 (2¹/₄-yard) lengths. Cut 1 piece in half lengthwise. Sew 1 narrow panel to each side of wide panel. Press seam allowances toward narrow panels.

2. Layer backing, batting, and quilt top; baste. Quilt as desired. Quilt shown was quilted in-the-ditch around appliqués and triangles. Blocks have grid and parallel quilting, and border features diagonal lines.

3. Join 2¹/₄"-wide green print strips for binding into 1 continuous strip to make straight-grain French-fold binding. Follow *Binding*, page 110, to add binding to quilt.

Border Appliqué Diagram

Appliqué patterns shown are finished size. Add $^1/_4$" seam allowance as
you cut out pieces for hand appliqué or cut along drawn lines for fusing.

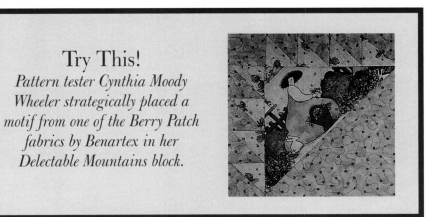

Try This!

Pattern tester Cynthia Moody Wheeler strategically placed a motif from one of the Berry Patch fabrics by Benartex in her Delectable Mountains block.

Trace, scan, or photocopy this quilt label to finish your quilt.

Blaze of Glory

QUILT BY LENA & ROY COLLEY (NEW TRADITIONS)

Finished Size: 84" x 96" (213 x 244 cm)
Blocks: 42 – 12" (30 cm) Memory Star Blocks

C ommemorate national holidays with an eye-catching tribute to Old Glory. Sure to spark a surge of patriotism, this stunning quilt combines a star-spangled background with Memory Star blocks to create a definite crowd-pleaser. If the colors are a bit too bold for your décor, try using muted red, white, and blue prints.

Materials

$2^1/4$ yards (2.1 m) white-on-white print for blocks and borders
$4^3/4$ yards (4.3 m) red print for blocks and borders
$4^3/4$ yards (4.3 m) blue print for blocks, borders, and binding
$7^1/2$ yards (6.9 m) 42" (107 cm) wide fabric for backing or 3 yards (2.7 m) 90" (229 cm) wide bleached muslin
Queen-size batting

Cutting

Each block has 57 pieces and many seams. Accuracy is required in cutting, piecing, and assembly in order for the block to measure $12^1/2$" when completed, including seam allowances. We strongly recommend pressing, measuring, and squaring (if needed) at each step in order to ensure proper size. Cut crosswise strips unless otherwise noted. Measurements include $1/4$" seam allowances. Follow *Rotary Cutting,* page 100.
From white-on-white print, cut:
- 8 ($1^1/2$"-wide) strips and piece as necessary to make 2 ($1^1/2$" x $84^1/2$") strips for side borders and 2 ($1^1/2$" x $74^1/2$") strips for top and bottom borders.
- 5 ($4^1/2$"-wide) strips. Cut strips into 42 ($4^1/2$") squares (A).
- 12 ($2^7/8$"-wide) strips. Cut strips into 168 ($2^7/8$") squares. Cut squares in half diagonally to make 336 half-square triangles (C).

From red print, cut:
- 9 ($2^1/2$"-wide) strips and piece as necessary to make 2 ($2^1/2$" x $86^1/2$") strips for side borders and 2 ($2^1/2$" x $78^1/2$") strips for top and bottom borders.
- 11 ($2^1/2$"-wide) strips. Cut strips into 168 ($2^1/2$") squares (B).
- 36 ($2^7/8$"-wide) strips. Cut strips into 504 ($2^7/8$") squares. Cut each square in half diagonally to make 1,008 half-square triangles (C).

From blue print, cut:
- 10 ($3^1/2$"-wide) strips and piece as necessary to make 2 ($3^1/2$" x $90^1/2$") strips for side borders and 2 ($3^1/2$" x $84^1/2$") strips for top and bottom borders.
- 11 ($2^1/2$"-wide) strips. Cut strips into 168 ($2^1/2$") squares (B).
- 24 ($2^7/8$"-wide) strips. Cut strips into 336 ($2^7/8$") squares. Cut squares in half diagonally to make 672 half-square triangles (C).
- 10 ($2^1/4$"-wide) strips for binding.

This large block will accommodate medium- and large-scale prints well. Any three-color combination will work. Since this pattern involves a lot of cutting and piecing, it's a good idea to assemble one test block before purchasing large amounts of fabric.

Block Assembly

1. Join 336 white Cs and red Cs in pairs along diagonal to make 336 triangle-squares.
2. Join remaining 672 red Cs and blue Cs along diagonal to make 672 triangle-squares.
3. Referring to *Block Assembly Diagram*, join Row 3 as shown. Then join pieces in 5 horizontal rows, pressing seam allowances in opposite directions from row to row. Join rows to make 42 Memory Star blocks *(Block Diagram.)*

Block Assembly Diagram

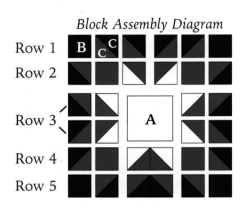

Block Diagram

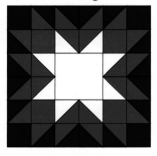

Quilt Assembly

1. Referring to *Quilt Top Diagram*, page 47, arrange blocks in 7 horizontal rows of 6 blocks each. Join blocks to make rows; join rows to complete inner quilt top.
2. Join 84$\frac{1}{2}$"-long white borders to sides of quilt. Add remaining white borders to quilt top and bottom. Add red and blue borders in the same manner.

Quilting and Finishing

1. Cut backing fabric into 3 (2$\frac{1}{2}$-yard) lengths. Join lengths to form backing. Seams on backing will run parallel to top and bottom of quilt edges.
2. Layer backing, batting, and quilt top; baste. Quilt as desired. Quilt shown was machine stipple quilted in matching thread.
3. Join 2$\frac{1}{4}$"-wide blue strips for binding into 1 continuous strip to make 11 yards of straight-grain French-fold binding. Follow *Binding*, page 110, to add binding to quilt.

Trace, scan, or photocopy this quilt label to finish your quilt.

Back in Time Stars

DESIGNED BY MARIANNE FONS & LIZ PORTER

Finished Size: 84" x 100" (213 x 254 cm)
Blocks: 50 – 8" (20 cm) Star Blocks

T his inviting quilt began as a classroom exercise. Marianne Fons won 16 star blocks in a class drawing, and she and Liz Porter added more before they assembled the quilt top in the traditional Straight Furrows setting. Although it was originally meant to be a lap-sized quilt, *Back in Time Stars* just kept growing when Marianne and Liz realized they liked the quilt so much that they couldn't stop.

Materials

Use plaids, checks, and stripes, as well as prints. The colors we used included cadet blue, navy, brown, red, maroon, gray, black, pink, gold, and green. Our light fabrics are shirting prints—prints with small, dark motifs on light backgrounds.—Marianne

80 ($2^1/2$" x 42") strips total [approximately $5^5/8$ yards (5.1 m)] of light, medium, and dark print fabrics for Star blocks

12 ($2^1/2$" x 21") strips total [approximately $1/2$ yard (46 cm)] of medium to dark print fabrics for pieced border

12 ($4^7/8$" x 21") strips total [approximately 1 yard (91 cm)] of medium to dark print fabrics for pieced border

13 ($2^7/8$" x 21") strips total [approximately $5/8$ yard (57 cm)] of medium to light print fabrics for pieced border

$3^1/2$ yards (3.2 m) of red print fabric for setting blocks, inner border, and binding

2 yards (1.8 m) of light plaid fabric for setting blocks

$7^1/2$ yards (6.9 m) of backing fabric

Queen-size batting

Cutting

Before cutting pieces, read instructions carefully. Make all cuts in crosswise strips. Measurements include $1/4$" seam allowances. Follow *Rotary Cutting*, page 100. When cutting pieces for Star blocks, cut only squares and rectangles. You'll use diagonal seams method to make star points.

From $2^1/2$" x 42" strips, cut following pieces for each of 50 blocks:

- 4 matching $2^1/2$" squares for corners.
- 2 sets of 2 matching $2^1/2$" squares for center four-patch.
- 8 matching $2^1/2$" squares for star points.
- 4 matching $2^1/2$" x $4^1/2$" rectangles.

From $2^1/2$" x 21" strips, cut:

- 88 ($2^1/2$") squares for border units.

From $4^7/8$"-wide strips, cut:

- 44 ($4^7/8$") squares. Cut squares in half diagonally to make 88 triangles for border units.

From $2^7/8$"-wide strips, cut:

- 88 ($2^7/8$") squares. Cut squares in half diagonally to make 176 triangles for border units.

From red print fabric, cut:

- 9 ($2^1/2$"-wide) strips for inner border.
- 7 ($8^7/8$"-wide) strips. From these, cut 25 ($8^7/8$") squares to make setting blocks.
- 10 ($2^1/4$"-wide) strips for binding.

From light plaid fabric, cut:

- 7 ($8^7/8$"-wide) strips. From these, cut 25 ($8^7/8$") squares to make setting blocks.

Quilt Assembly

1. Referring to *Block Piecing Diagram,* for each block select 2 pairs of matching squares for center Four-patch (A), 4 matching squares for corners (B), 8 matching squares for star points (C), and 4 matching rectangles for sides (D).

Block Piecing Diagram

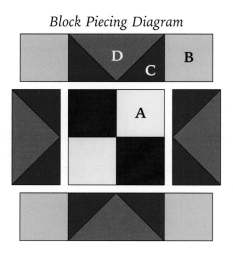

2. Referring to *Diagonal Seams Diagrams,* lay 1 C on end of 1 D, with right sides facing, as shown in *Step 1.*

Diagonal Seams Diagram, Step 1

3. Stitch from corner to corner as shown in *Step 2.* Trim $1/4$" from stitching. Open triangle and press seam allowances toward C.

Diagonal Seams Diagram, Step 2

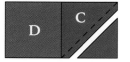

4. Referring to *Step 3,* lay 1 matching C on remaining end of D. Stitch as shown. Trim and press as before to make completed side unit shown in *Step 4.* Make 4 matching side units for each block.

Diagonal Seams Diagram, Step 3

Diagonal Seams Diagram, Step 4

5. Referring to *Block Piecing Diagram* lay out 4 squares for center Four-patch, 4 side units, and 4 corner squares.

6. Join center squares into 2 rows of 2 squares each. Press seam allowances in opposite directions. Join rows to complete Four-patch unit.

7. Sew 2 side units to opposite sides of Four-patch as shown to complete center row of Star block. Press seam allowances toward Four-patch.

8. Sew squares to opposite ends of remaining side units as shown. Press seam allowances toward squares. Sew units to top and bottom of center row as shown. Press seam allowances toward top and bottom. Repeat to make total of 50 Star blocks.

Give your quilt zest by making a few Maverick Blocks (page 53). – Marianne

9. Referring to *Setting Block Diagrams*, page 51, place 1 red print square and 1 light plaid square with right sides facing. Draw diagonal line from 1 corner to another as shown.

10. Stitch ¹/₄" on each side of drawn line as shown. Cut on drawn line. Open triangles and press seam allowances toward darker fabric. You will have 2 setting blocks. Repeat to make a total of 49 setting blocks plus 1 extra.

Setting Block Diagrams

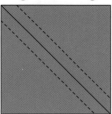

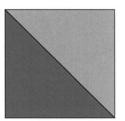

11. Referring to *Quilt Top Diagram*, page 52, lay out Star blocks and setting blocks in 11 horizontal rows of 9 blocks each, alternating blocks as shown and noting placement of dark and light halves of setting blocks.

12. Join blocks in each row. Press seam allowances toward setting blocks. Join rows to complete inner quilt.

13. Using diagonal seams *(Diagram A)*, join pairs of red print border strips to make 4 borders. Cut remaining strip in half. Sew 1 half-strip to each of 2 border strips to make side borders.

Diagram A

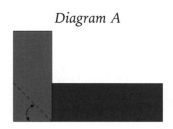

14. Trim 2 longer borders to 88¹/₂" long and 2 shorter borders to 76¹/₂" long. Sew longer borders to quilt sides. Press seam allowances toward borders. Sew shorter borders to top and bottom edges; press.

15. Referring to the *Border Unit Diagram*, lay out 1 large triangle, 2 small triangles, and 1 square to form unit.

Border Unit Diagram

16. Sew 1 leg of small triangles to adjacent sides of square to form pieced triangle unit as shown. Press seam allowances toward small triangles. Sew large triangle to pieced triangle unit. Press seam allowances toward large triangle. Repeat to make total of 88 border units.

17. Referring to *Quilt Top Diagram*, join units into 2 borders of 23 units each, noting placement of squares. Press seam allowances toward dark triangles. Sew borders to sides of quilt. In same manner, join remaining units into 2 borders of 21 units each; press. Sew borders to top and bottom of quilt.

Quilting and Finishing

1. Mark desired quilting designs on quilt top. Quilt shown was utility quilted in 2" grid.

2. Cut backing fabric into 3 (2½-yard) lengths. Join lengths to form backing. Seams on backing will run parallel to top and bottom of quilt edges.

3. Layer backing, batting, and quilt top; baste. Quilt as desired.

4. Join 2¼"-wide red print strips for binding into 1 continuous strip to make straight-grain French-fold binding. Follow *Binding*, page 110, to add binding to quilt.

Quilt Top Diagram

Maverick Blocks

One of our favorite characteristics of late 19th-century scrap quilts is the presence of what we call "maverick blocks."

Many old quilts have rows and rows of normal-looking patchwork blocks, and then suddenly you see a very odd one, with the lights and darks arranged so differently that the block seems to be a different pattern. *Maverick* is our term for these blocks that don't fit the norm.

Take a look at *Back in Time Stars*. We had so much fun making maverick blocks that they almost became normal!

Notice how the star design is very obvious (normal) in blocks that have bright or dark star points with light fabrics next to them *(photo A)*. In others, the star points are less evident because of how we matched the light and dark pieces. For example, in some, darker fabrics form a diagonal cross through the blocks *(photo B)*; in others, the darker fabrics run through the vertical and horizontal centers *(photo C)*.

Quiltmakers of the past often took a rather cavalier approach to choosing lights and darks for their patchwork. They plucked snippets from scrap bags and produced blocks that could not have come from a kit. We have a lot of fun making maverick blocks and have come to view them as a key ingredient in our old-style quilts.

How many maverick blocks do you find in Back in Time Stars? *(We counted 30.)*

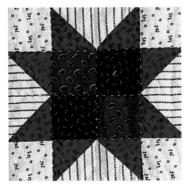

A. Normal Star Block

B. Maverick Block
(diagonal cross)

C. Maverick Block
(up-and-down cross)

Marianne's inspiration for *Stars and Crosses* came from a photo of an antique quilt made around 1800. "The Album Cross and Sawtooth Star are blocks I've made many times before," says Marianne. "But I wanted to try the effect using the same light gold print for the star backgrounds in one block and the crossbars in the other. I love the lattice result."

Materials

25 fat quarters* assorted dark prints for Sawtooth Star blocks and border
3 yards (2.7 m) brown print for Album Cross blocks and binding
3/8 yard (34 cm) yellow floral for Album Cross blocks
6 3/4 yards (6.2 m) yellow print for background and border
7 1/2 yards (6.9 m) fabric for backing
Queen-size batting
12" or 12 1/2" square ruler
*Fat quarter = 18" x 22" (46 x 56 cm)

Cutting

Measurements include 1/4" seam allowances. Cut crosswise strips unless otherwise noted. Border strips are exact length needed so outer pieced border will fit. Follow *Rotary Cutting*, page 100.

From each dark fat quarter, cut:
- 1 (5 1/4"-wide) strip. Cut strip into 2 (5 1/4") squares. Cut squares in quarters diagonally to make 8 quarter-square triangles (G) for border blocks. You will have 24 extra.
- 1 (4 1/2"-wide) strip. Cut strip into 2 (4 1/2") squares (C).
- 3 (2 1/2"-wide) strips. Cut strips into 16 (2 1/2") squares for Sawtooth Star blocks (A).

From brown print, cut:
- 10 (7 1/2"-wide) strips. Cut strips into 49 (7 1/2") squares. Cut squares in quarters diagonally to make 196 triangles (F) for Album Cross blocks.
- 10 (2 1/4"-wide) strips for binding.

From yellow floral, cut:
- 4 (2 1/2"-wide) strips. Cut strips into 49 (2 1/2") squares for Album Cross blocks (E).

From yellow print, cut:
- 9 (2 1/2"-wide) strips. Piece to make 2 (2 1/2" x 88 1/2") side inner borders and 2 (2 1/2" x 76 1/2") top and bottom inner borders.
- 7 (5 1/4"-wide) strips. Cut strips into 44 (5 1/4") squares. Cut squares in quarters diagonally to make 176 quarter-square triangles for outer border (G).
- 13 (2 1/2"-wide) strips. Cut strips into 200 (2 1/2") squares (A) for Sawtooth Star blocks.
- 28 (2 1/2"-wide) strips. Cut strips into 196 (2 1/2" x 5 1/2") rectangles (D) for Album Cross blocks.
- 23 (2 1/2"-wide) strips. Cut strips into 200 (2 1/2" x 4 1/2") rectangles (B) for Sawtooth Star blocks.

Star Block Assembly

1. Referring to *Diagonal Seams Diagrams,* lay 1 dark A atop 1 end of 1 background B rectangle. Sew diagonally, trim, fold out, and press. Repeat on opposite end to make 1 Goose Chase unit. Make 4 matching Goose Chase units.

Diagonal Seams Diagram

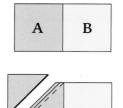

2. Referring to *Sawtooth Star Block Assembly Diagram,* join 1 Goose Chase unit to opposite sides of 1 matching dark C square.
3. Join 1 background A square to each end of remaining Goose Chase units. Add to top and bottom to complete block (*Sawtooth Star Block Diagram*).
4. Make 50 Sawtooth Star blocks.

Sawtooth Star Block Assembly Diagram

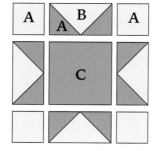

Sawtooth Star Block Diagram

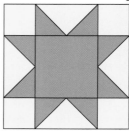

Album Cross Block Assembly

1. Referring to *Album Cross Block Assembly Diagram,* arrange pieces for 1 block as shown. Join 1 E between 2 Ds. Join 1 F to each side of remaining 2 Ds.
   Note: Triangles are oversize and cross rectangles are longer than needed. You will trim these to size later. Match the right angle (square corner) of triangle to end of D rectangle. Take care not to stretch them as you sew and press!

Album Cross Block Assembly Diagram

2. From typing paper, cut a $1^7/_8$" square. Referring to *Cutting Diagram*, alight 2 adjacent corners of paper square with $4^1/_4$" marks on square ruler. Tape square to ruler.

Cutting Diagram

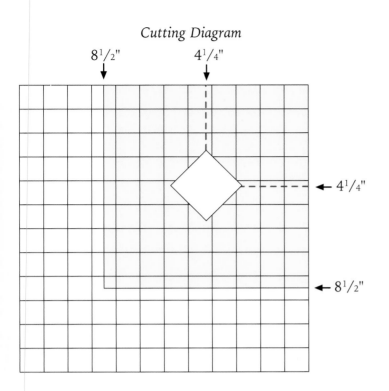

3. Place prepared rotary-cutting square over block, aligning paper square over block center (E). Trim 2 sides. Turn block and reposition ruler so that trimmed edges align with $8^1/_2$" marks and then trim remaining 2 sides. This method ensures that your center square is centered and that block measures $8^1/_2$" *(Album Cross Block Diagram)*.

4. Make 49 Album Cross blocks.

Album Cross Block Diagram

Border Block Assembly

1. Choose 2 background G triangles and 2 matching dark G triangles. Join 1 of each as shown in *Border Block Assembly Diagram*. Repeat.
2. Join 2 units to complete 1 quarter-square triangle border block *(Border Block Diagram)*.
3. Make 88 border blocks.

Border Block Assembly Diagram

Border Block Diagram

57

Quilt Assembly

1. Referring to *Quilt Top Assembly Diagram*, page 59, lay out blocks in 11 horizontal rows of 9 blocks each, alternating Sawtooth Star and Album Cross blocks as shown. Join into rows; join rows to complete center.
2. Add 2¹/₂" x 88¹/₂" yellow print borders to quilt sides. Press seam allowance toward borders. Add 2¹/₂" x 86¹/₂" top and bottom borders.
3. Join 23 border blocks into 1 side border strip, rotating blocks as shown. Add to quilt. Repeat for opposite side.
4. Join 21 border blocks into 1 top border strip, rotating blocks as shown. Add to top of quilt. Repeat for bottom border.

Quilting and Finishing

1. Cut backing fabric into 3 (2¹/₂-yard) lengths. Cut 1 piece in half lengthwise. Sew 1 narrow panel between wide panels. Press seams allowances toward narrow panel. Seams will run horizontally. Remaining narrow panel is extra.
2. Layer backing, batting, and quilt top; baste. Quilt as desired. Quilt shown was quilted in-the-ditch in blocks. Sawtooth Star blocks have a clamshell pattern in center section, and background areas have a vine pattern extending into borders.
3. Join 2¹/₄"-wide brown print strips for binding into 1 continuous strip to make straight-grain French-fold binding. Follow *Binding*, page 110, to add binding to quilt.

Try This!
If a reproduction look does not fit into your home décor, try matching fabrics to your bedroom. Here, pattern tester Pat Myers used a contemporary yellow-and-blue color scheme.

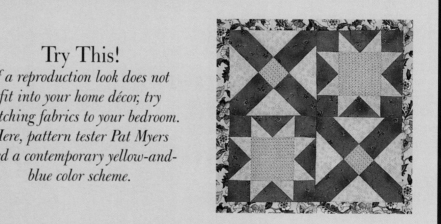

Stars in the Forest

QUILT BY JULIE LARSEN FOR PRAIRIE DESIGNS

Finished Size: 85" x 100" (216 x 254 cm)
Blocks: 20 – 15" (38 cm) Combination Star Blocks and
36 – 7½" (19 cm) Tree Blocks

F or projects to keep them busy at the annual Runaway Quilters Retreat in Elk Horn, Iowa, teaching partners Sharlot Steen, Pam Kuehl, and Julie Larsen chose the Combination Star block. *Stars in the Forest* is Julie's version. Muted colors and Tree blocks add an endearing touch to this simple quilt.

Materials
2³⁄₄ yards (2.5 m) red plaid for star centers and border
1¹⁄₂ yards (1.4 m) red print for star points
2⁷⁄₈ yards (2.6 m) gold print for background
1¹⁄₄ yards (1.1 m) green plaid for blocks
1 yard (91 cm) light cream prints for blocks
2³⁄₄ yards (2.5 m) light green print for blocks
2¹⁄₂ yards (2.3 m) green pinecone print for trees
³⁄₄ yard (69 cm) red print for binding
7¹⁄₂ yards (6.9 m) fabric for backing
Queen-size batting
Freezer paper for templates

Cutting
Measurements include ¹⁄₄" seam allowances. Cut crosswise strips unless otherwise noted. Border strips are exact length needed. You may want to cut them longer to allow for piecing variations. Follow *Rotary Cutting*, page 100.

From red plaid, cut:
- 4 (5¹⁄₂"-wide) lengthwise strips. Trim strips to make 2 (5¹⁄₂" x 90¹⁄₂") side borders and 2 (5¹⁄₂" x 85¹⁄₂") top and bottom borders.
- From remainder, cut:
  - 7 (5¹⁄₂"-wide) crosswise strips. Cut strips into 20 (5¹⁄₂") A squares for star centers.
  - 4 (3") F squares for corner blocks.

From red print, cut:
- 7 (6¹⁄₄"-wide) strips. Cut strips into 40 (6¹⁄₄") squares. Cut squares in quarters diagonally to make 160 D quarter-square triangles for star points.

From gold print, cut:
- 18 (3"-wide) strips. Cut strips into 252 (3") C squares.
- 6 (6¹⁄₄"-wide) strips. Cut strips into 36 (6¹⁄₄") squares. Cut squares in quarters diagonally to make 144 D quarter-square triangles for star points. You will have 2 extra.

From green plaid, cut:
- 7 (5¹⁄₂"-wide) strips. Cut strips into 48 (5¹⁄₂") B squares.
- 4 (3³⁄₈") squares. Cut squares in half diagonally to make 8 half-square triangles I for corner blocks.

From light cream print, cut:
- 5 (5¹⁄₂"-wide) strips. Cut strips into 32 (5¹⁄₂") B squares.
- 1 (3"-wide) strip. Cut strip into 12 (3") F squares for corner blocks.

From freezer paper, cut:
- 36 (2¹⁄₂") squares. Fold squares in half. Cut paper on diagonal from top folded corner to bottom loose corners to make 1 G, 1 H, and 1 H reversed piecing templates from each square.

From light green print, cut:
- 5 (3"-wide) strips. Cut strips into 68 (3") C squares for star blocks.
- 1 (6¼" wide) strip. Cut strip into 5 (6¼") squares. Cut squares in quarters diagonally to make 20 D quarter-square triangles. You will have 2 extra.
- 3 (3½"-wide) strips. Press freezer paper H and H reversed templates to wrong side of fabric, leaving ½" between templates. Cut apart with rotary cutter, leaving ¼" seam allowances on all sides.
- 16 (3"-wide) strips. Cut strips into 220 (3") F squares for tree blocks and corner blocks.
- 1 (3⅜"-wide) strip. Cut strip into 4 (3⅜") squares. Cut squares in half diagonally to make 8 I half-square triangles for corner blocks.

From green pinecone print, cut:
- 3 (3½"-wide) strips. Press freezer paper G templates to wrong side of fabric, leaving ½" between templates. Cut apart with rotary cutter, leaving ¼" seam allowance on all sides.
- 15 (3"-wide) strips. Cut strips into 72 (3" x 8") E rectangles for tree blocks.
- 1 (3"-wide) strip. Cut strip into 8 (3") F squares for corner blocks.

From red print, cut:
- 10 (2¼"-wide) strips for binding.

Square-in-a-Square Unit Assembly

1. Referring to *Diagonal Seams Diagrams*, place 1 gold C atop 1 corner of 1 green plaid B. Stitch diagonally from corner to corner. Trim excess fabric ¼" beyond stitching. Press open to reveal triangle. Repeat on each corner to make 1 green Square-in-a-Square unit. Make 48 green units.

Diagonal Seams Diagrams

2. Repeat to make 1 edge Square-in-a-Square unit with 2 light green Cs and 2 gold Cs on 1 light cream B as shown. Make 28 edge units.
3. Repeat to make 1 corner Square-in-a-Square unit with 3 light green Cs and 1 gold C on 1 light cream B. Make 4 corner units.

Square-in-a-Square Units

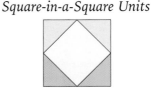

Green Units
Make 48.

Edge Units
Make 28.

Corner Units
Make 4.

Quarter-Square Unit Assembly

1. Lay out 2 red Ds and 2 gold Ds as shown in *Quarter-Square Unit Assembly Diagram*. Join to make 1 inner star point. Make 62 inner star point units.
2. Repeat to make 1 outer star point unit with 2 red Ds, 1 gold D, and 1 light green D as shown. Make 18 outer star point units.

Quarter-Square Unit Assembly Diagram

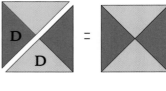

Inner Star
Point Unit
Make 62.

Outer Star
Point Unit
Make 18.

Star Block Assembly

1. Referring to *Inner Star Block Assembly Diagram,* lay out 4 green units, 4 inner star point units, and 1 red plaid A. Join into rows; join rows to complete 1 Inner Star block. Make 6 Inner Star blocks.

Inner Star Block Assembly Diagram

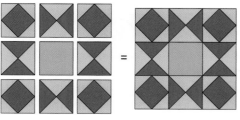

2. Referring to *Outer Star Block Assembly Diagram,* lay out 2 green units, 2 edge units, 3 inner star point units, 1 outer star point unit, and 1 red plaid A. Join into rows; join rows to complete 1 Outer Star block. Make 10 Outer Star blocks.

Outer Star Block Assembly Diagram

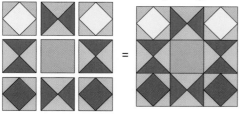

3. Referring to *Corner Star Block Assembly Diagram,* lay out 1 green unit, 1 corner unit, 2 edge units, 2 inner star point units, 2 outer star point units, and 1 red plaid A. Join into rows; join rows to complete 1 Corner Star block. Make 4 Corner Star blocks.

Corner Star Block Assembly Diagram

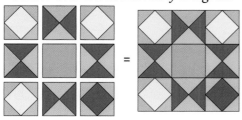

Tree Block Assembly

1. Align corners of freezer paper/fabric piece at top and bottom of G and H. Sew along long edge of paper. Repeat on opposite side. Remove freezer paper to make 1 tree top unit. Add 1 light green F square to each side of unit *(Tree Top Unit Diagram).*

Tree Top Unit Diagram

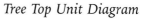

2. Using diagonal seams, place 1 F square atop 1 end of 1 E rectangle. Stitch diagonally from corner to corner. Trim excess fabric ¹⁄₄" beyond stitching. Press open to reveal triangle. Repeat on opposite end to make 1 tree base unit *(Tree Base Unit Diagram).* Make 2 tree base units.

Tree Base Unit Diagram

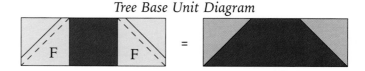

3. Referring to *Tree Block Assembly Diagram,* join 1 tree top unit and 2 tree base units to complete 1 Tree block.
4. Make 36 Tree blocks.

Tree Block Assembly Diagram

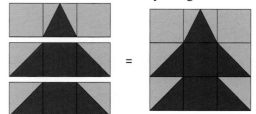

Corner Block Assembly

1. Join 1 light green I and 1 green plaid I as shown. Repeat to make 2 half-square triangle units.
2. Lay out 2 half-square triangle units, 3 light cream Fs, 1 light green F, 2 green pinecone Fs, and 1 red plaid F as shown in *Corner Border Block Assembly Diagram*. Join into rows; join rows to complete 1 Corner block.
3. Make 4 Corner blocks.

Corner Border Block Assembly Diagram

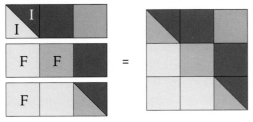

Quilt Assembly

1. Carefully following *Quilt Top Assembly Diagram*, page 65, lay out blocks as shown. Join blocks into rows; join rows to complete quilt center.
2. Add 1 red plaid ($5^{1}/_{2}$" x $90^{1}/_{2}$") side border to each side of quilt. Add top and bottom red plaid ($5^{1}/_{2}$" x $85^{1}/_{2}$") borders to quilt.

Quilting and Finishing

1. Divide backing fabric into 3 ($2^{1}/_{2}$-yard) lengths. Join panels to make backing. Seams will run horizontally.
2. Layer backing, batting, and quilt top; baste. Quilt as desired. Quilt shown was meander-quilted in stars, with tight loops in the outer light blocks. Trees have a looped pattern, with pine needle sprays quilted into the backgrounds. Outer border features stars surrounded by meander quilting.
3. Join $2^{1}/_{4}$"-wide red print strips for binding into 1 continuous strip to make straight-grain French-fold binding. Follow *Binding*, page 110, to add binding to quilt.

Trace, scan, or photocopy this quilt label to finish your quilt.

Try This!

Pattern tester Cynthia Moody Wheeler decided to make her blocks less seasonal by using Tradewinds fabrics by Maywood Studios. The green and purple fabrics are by Moda.

Flying Geese

ANTIQUE QUILT FROM THE COLLECTION OF LIZ PORTER AND MARIANNE FONS

Finished Size: 92" width x 86" height (234 x 218 cm)
Blocks: 473 - 4" x 2" (10 x 5 cm) Flying Geese Blocks

I f you are a collector of antique quilts, you've probably experienced the phenomenon of having a quilt "talk" to you and tell you it wants to come home with you. This quilt "talked" to Marianne and Liz while they shopped the merchant's mall at the 1996 Quilter's Heritage Celebration in Lancaster, Pennsylvania. The bright red calico with chrome yellow flowers is typical of quilts found in that area.

Materials

Dark scraps totaling 4 yards (3.7 m) for Flying Geese [approximately ¼ yard (23 cm) each of 5 reds, 5 blues, and 6 assorted greens, browns, and plaids]
Light scraps totaling 4⅝ yards (4.2 m) for background
5 yards (4.6 m) red print for sashing strips
8⅜ yards (7.7 m) plaid for backing
Queen-size batting

Cutting

Measurements include ¼" seam allowances. Cut crosswise strips unless otherwise noted. Sashing strips are cut lengthwise and call for exact length needed; you may want to cut them longer to allow for piecing variations. Follow *Rotary Cutting*, page 100.
From assorted dark scraps, cut:
• 53 (2½"-wide) strips. Cut strips into 473 (2½" x 4½") rectangles.
From assorted light scraps, cut:
• 60 (2½"-wide) strips. Cut strips into 946 (2½") squares.
From red print, cut:
• 2 (2½ yard) lengths. From these, cut 12 (4½" x 86½") lengthwise strips.

Block Assembly

1. Place 1 (2½") light square on 1 end of a 2½" x 4½" dark rectangle. Stitch diagonally across square (*Diagram 1*). Trim excess and press seam allowance toward small triangle (*Diagram 2*). Repeat on opposite end of rectangle to complete Flying Geese block (*Diagrams 3 and 4*).

Diagram 1

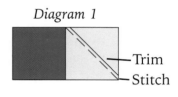

Diagram 2

Diagram 3

Diagram 4

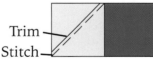

2. Repeat to make 473 Flying Geese blocks.

Quilt Assembly

1. Referring to photo and to *Row Assembly Diagram*, arrange blocks in 11 strips of 43 blocks each. Join to complete Flying Geese rows.

Row Assembly Diagram

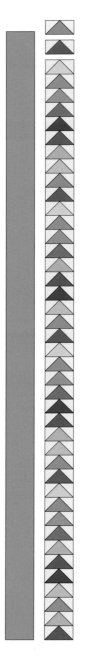

This quilt would make a great cutting bee quilt. Invite five of your friends to have a cutting bee to collect a wide assortment of medium and dark fabrics for this quilt. Ask each person to bring an assortment of light, medium, and dark-print fabrics to cut into 2¹/₂"-wide strips, rotary-cutting equipment, and a covered dish for a potluck dinner. If you each cut a total of 54 medium/dark strips and trade sets of nine strips with the others in the group, you will have 54 different strips to cut the "geese" for this quilt and have great fun doing it! Cut 60 light strips and trade sets of 10. —Liz

To keep the Goose Chase blocks even from row to row, make positioning marks on the wrong side of the red strips. —Liz

2. Alternate Flying Geese rows with red sashing strips as shown. Join rows vertically to complete quilt top.

Quilting and Finishing

Diagram 6

1. Referring to Diagram 5, cut backing into 3 (2³/₄-yard) pieces. Join along long sides to make backing so that seams are parallel to top and bottom of quilt. Trim backing to 99"-wide x 95"-long, keeping middle panel centered.

Diagram 5

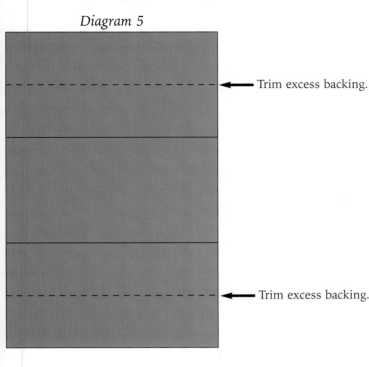

← Trim excess backing.

← Trim excess backing.

2. Layer backing, batting, and quilt top. Baste. Quilt as desired. Quilt shown was quilted in reverse Vs in each block (*Diagram 6*) with diagonal lines in sashing strips.

3. Quilt shown has self-binding. To do this, trim batting ¹/₄" larger than quilt top. Trim backing around quilt top so that it extends 1" around all edges. Press a fold in excess backing so that backing extends ¹/₂". Fold backing to front to make ¹/₄"-wide binding; slipstitch in place. If you prefer a separate binding, use excess backing or red fabric to make 380" of 2 ¹/₄"-wide French-fold straight-grain binding. Follow *Binding*, page 110, to add binding to quilt.

> *To keep crisp points on the Goose Chase blocks, stack units so that the one on top has its tip pointing toward the needle as you feed it through the sewing machine. Stitch through the X of stitching that was made when you constructed the block.* —Marianne

Trace, scan, or photocopy this quilt label to finish your quilt.

North Winds Weathervane

DESIGNED BY MARIANNE FONS AND LIZ PORTER; MADE BY MARIANNE FONS

Finished Size: 82" x 99" (208 x 251 cm)
Blocks: 22 - 12" (30 cm) squares

Marianne and Liz started this handsome quilt at Liz's house during a flannel cutting bee they hosted one fall. Liz cut all the pieces for the blocks, and Marianne machine-pieced them. Even before she finished *North Winds Weathervane*, Marianne often caught family members snuggling under the cozy quilt. "Everyone loves flannel quilts," Marianne says. "They make you want to curl up and take a nap."

Materials

1 ($2^7/8$" x 42") strip and 1 ($4^1/2$" x 42") strip each of 22 assorted medium/dark plaids or prints for patchwork blocks
8 ($2^1/2$" x 42") strips of red plaid or print for inner border
2 yards (1.8 m) of solid beige for block backgrounds
5 yards (4.6 m) of dark blue-and-green plaid for setting triangles, outer border, and binding
$7^1/2$ yards (6.9 m) of backing fabric
Queen-size batting

Cutting

Cut only squares and triangles to make these blocks. — Marianne

Measurements include $1/4$" seam allowances. Follow *Rotary Cutting*, page 100.
From each $2^7/8$"-wide medium/dark strip, cut:
- 4 ($2^7/8$") squares. Cut each square in half diagonally to get 2 triangles. Repeat for each strip to get 22 sets of 8 matching triangles (176 total).
- After cutting triangles, trim strip to $2^1/2$" wide and cut 4 matching $2^1/2$" squares from each strip.
From each $4^1/2$"-wide medium/dark strip, cut:
- 4 ($4^1/2$") squares (22 sets of 4, or 88 squares total).
- 1 ($4^1/2$") square (22 total) for block centers. Center squares can match or contrast with small squares and triangles in each block.
From beige, cut:
- 7 ($2^7/8$" x 42") strips. From these, cut 88 ($2^7/8$") squares. Cut each square in half diagonally to make 2 triangles (176 triangles total).

- 17 ($2^1/2$" x 42") strips. From these, cut 264 ($2^1/2$") squares.
From dark blue-and-green plaid, cut:
- 1 ($9^3/8$" x 42") strip. From this, cut 4 ($9^3/8$") squares. Cut each square in half diagonally to make 8 Z setting triangles.
- 5 ($18^1/4$" x 42") strips. From strips, cut 9 ($18^1/4$") squares. Cut each square in quarters diagonally to make 4 Y setting triangles (36 Y setting triangles total).
- 10 ($5^1/2$" x 42") border strips.

Block Assembly

1. Referring to *Block Diagram*, choose pieces for 1 block. For each block, choose 8 plaid triangles and 4 small plaid squares from same fabric, 4 large squares from another fabric, 1 large center square, 8 beige triangles, and 12 beige squares. *Note: Center square can match or contrast with small plaid triangles.*

Block Diagram

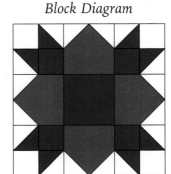

71

2. Referring to *Diagonal Seams Diagrams*, make 4 center side units as follows. With right sides facing, place 1 beige square on top of large plaid square as shown in Fig. 1. Stitch diagonally from corner to corner of small square. Trim off excess corner, leaving seam allowance, as shown in Fig. 2. Open triangle to right side as shown in Fig. 3. Press seam allowances toward triangle. In same manner, place second beige square on adjacent corner of large square; stitch, trim, and open triangle to complete unit (Figs. 4 and 5). Make total of 4 identical units.

Diagonal Seams Diagrams

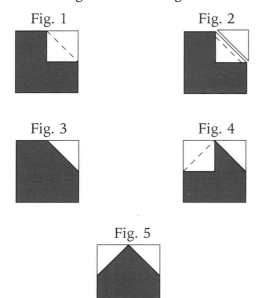

3. Join 1 beige triangle and 1 plaid triangle along long edges to make a triangle-square. Repeat with matching pieces to make a total of 8 identical triangle-squares.

4. Referring to *Corner Unit Diagram*, lay out 2 triangle-square units, 1 beige square, and 1 plaid square as shown. Join pieces to make 2 rows. Press seam allowances toward squares. Join rows to complete unit. Repeat to make 4 identical corner units.

Corner Unit Diagram

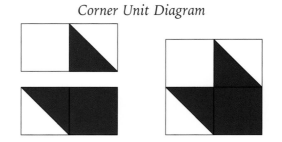

5. Referring to *Block Assembly Diagram*, lay out 4 center side units, 4 corner units, and 1 large center square. Join units as shown to make 3 rows. Press seam allowances away from corner units and center square. Join rows to complete block.

Block Assembly Diagram

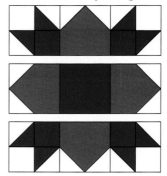

6. Repeat to make a total of 22 blocks.

Quilt Assembly

1. Lay out blocks, Y setting triangles, and Z setting triangles in 4 vertical rows as shown in *Quilt Top Assembly Diagram*, page 74.

2. Join blocks and setting triangles in diagonal rows (*Row Assembly Diagram*, page 74). Press seam allowances toward triangles. Join units to make rows.

3. If needed, place acrylic ruler on right sides of rows and trim setting pieces so that $1/4$" seam allowances are even along sides and at corners of rows. Join rows.

4. Use ruler and pencil to draw horizontal line through center of 4 extended blocks in second and fourth rows so that top and bottom edges will be even, allowing $1/4$" for seam allowances. Do not trim blocks yet.

5. Cut red border strips into random lengths, 6" to 27" long.

6. Measure length across center of quilt top (not along edges). Join assorted strips end-to-end to make 2 side borders equal to that measurement. Sew borders to sides of quilt. Press seam allowances toward borders.

7. Measure width across center of quilt, including borders. Join assorted border strips end-to-end to make top and bottom borders equal to that measurement. Sew borders to top and bottom of quilt top. Press seam allowances toward borders. Trim along drawn line through center of extended blocks, being careful not to cut borders.

8. Join dark plaid border strips to make 4 (95"-long) borders. Measure quilt, trim borders, and sew to quilt top in same manner as for inner borders.

Quilting and Finishing

1. Mark desired quilting designs on quilt top if necessary. Quilt shown was quilted with tan pearl cotton.

2. Divide backing fabric into 3 (90") lengths. Join panels. Press seam allowances in 1 direction.

3. Layer backing, batting, and quilt top; baste. Seams of backing run parallel to top and bottom edges of quilt. Quilt as desired.

4. Make 375" of straight-grain binding. Follow *Binding,* page 110, to add binding to quilt.

Trace, scan, or photocopy this quilt label to finish your quilt.

Quilting with Flannel

*Flannel fabrics are easy to work with, but they do behave
a bit differently than regular cotton broadcloth fabrics.*

Keep the following tips in mind when using flannel.

• Buy extra fabric. Flannels shrink and fray more when prewashed and dried than do most broadcloths.

• Prewash flannels and dry in a hot dryer before cutting. Wash dark colors separately.

• Most flannels accept dye easily, since they're not perma-press treated. Tea-dye or over-dye flannels to tone down contrast and age them. Follow dye package instructions.

• If patterns such as plaids pull out of shape during prewashing, pull on opposite corners of the fabric piece to realign the threads and straighten woven plaids. Enlist a friend or family member to tug on large pieces of fabric. Don't despair if you can't get a plaid perfectly straight. Plaids running at crazy angles add to the charm of your quilt.

• Treat the napped (fuzzy) side of flannel as the fabric right side when cutting and stitching.

• Use a slightly longer than normal stitch length ($2^1/_2$ to 3 on European machines or 10 to 12 stitches per inch) when piecing. The normal quilt piecing stitch length (12 to 15 stitches per inch) tends to stretch flannel, and the stitches become embedded in flannel's loose weave. A longer stitch length reduces stretching and makes ripping out seams easier.

• Use quick-piecing methods such as strip piecing and diagonal seams whenever possible. Larger fabric pieces make stretching easier to control, and quick-piecing methods reduce the number of small pieces you handle.

• Choose fairly simple blocks with basic patchwork shapes such as squares and triangles. Avoid working with tiny pieces. If you want to use a complex pattern, make the blocks larger than you otherwise might.

• Take extra care when pressing patchwork to avoid stretching pieces out of shape.

• Use flannel's extra give or stretchiness to your advantage when matching patchwork pieces. Sometimes you can stretch a slightly smaller piece to fit a larger one. To ease a larger piece to fit a smaller one, place the larger piece on bottom as you sew to allow the machine's feed dogs to help ease the piece to fit.

• Include low-contrast plaids and solid colors in your patchwork to help calm busier plaids.

• Since flannel fabrics are heavier than regular cotton fabrics, use low-loft polyester or cotton batting, or a layer of flannel as a filler for your quilt.

• When quilting flannel, make longer stitches. Flannel is easy to quilt because it is more loosely woven than regular cotton broadcloth. Tiny quilting stitches tend to disappear into flannel's loose weave.

• Try utility quilting using pearl cotton or crochet thread and a crewel needle. Utility quilting stitches should be $1/_8$" to $1/_4$" long with even spacing between stitches. Primitive or crude in appearance, utility quilting seems to fit the mood of flannel quilts.

• Clean and oil your sewing machine frequently because sewing flannels produces more lint around the feed dogs.

Dutchman's Puzzle

QUILT BY LIZ PORTER; HAND-QUILTED BY CORA YODER

Finished Size: 44" x 55¹/₈" (112 x 140 cm)
Blocks: 12 - 8" (20 cm) Dutchman's Puzzle Blocks

After inheriting some leftover strips from a flannel cutting bee, Liz decided to use the strips to piece this rustic baby quilt. "To give the blocks some uniformity, I began by cutting pieces for the blocks from the longest strips. Then I used a variety of leftover strips to make the string-pieced border," Liz says.

Materials

24 (2½" x 42") strips of assorted medium/dark prints for blocks and border
14 (2½" x 42") strips of assorted light prints for blocks and border
1 yard (91 cm) cranberry-and-black check for setting squares and triangles
¼ yard (23 cm) solid black for inner border
½ yard (46 cm) fabric for binding
3 yards (2.7 m) fabric for backing
48" x 60" (122 x 152 cm) piece of batting

Cutting

Measurements include ¼" seam allowances. Cut crosswise strips unless otherwise noted. Follow *Rotary Cutting*, page 100.

From each assorted medium/dark strip, cut:
• 4 matching 2½" x 4½" rectangles. Reserve remaining half-strips for use in border.

From each of 12 assorted light strips, cut:
• 16 matching 2½" squares. Reserve remaining 2 strips for use in borders.

From cranberry-and-black check, cut:
• 2 (8½"-wide) strips. Cut strips into:
  • 6 (8½") setting squares (X).
  • 2 (6⅝") squares. Cut squares in half diagonally to make 4 corner triangles (Z).
• 1 (12⅝"-wide) strip. Cut strip into 3 (12⅝") squares. Cut squares in quarters diagonally to make 12 setting triangles (Y). You will have 2 extra.

From solid black, cut:
• 5 (1½"-wide) strips for inner border.

From binding fabric, cut:
• 6 (2½"-wide) strips for binding.

Block Assembly

1. Referring to *Block Assembly Diagram,* select 2 sets of 4 matching medium/dark rectangles for large triangles and 1 set of 16 matching 2½" light squares for background. 2. Referring to *Diagonal Seams Diagrams,* place 1 light square atop 1 end of medium/dark rectangle, with right sides facing, as shown in Step A. Stitch diagonally and trim excess fabric ¼" beyond stitching as shown in Step B.

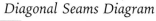

Diagonal Seams Diagram

Step A　　Step B　　Step C　　Step D

3. Open triangle and press as shown in Step C.
4. Place another square atop other end of rectangle. Stitch and trim as shown in Step C. Trim excess.
5. Press open to reveal Goose Chase unit as shown in Step D. Repeat to make 2 sets of 4 matching Goose Chase units.
6. Referring to *Block Assembly Diagram,* arrange units as shown. Join units to form quadrants; join quadrants to complete block.
7. Repeat to make 12 blocks.

Block Assembly Diagram

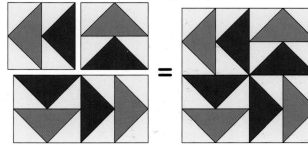

Quilt Assembly

1. Referring to *Quilt Top Assembly Diagram,* lay out pieces as shown.
2. Join blocks and setting pieces in diagonal rows. Press seam allowances toward setting pieces. Join rows; press seam allowances to 1 side.
3. Cut 1 (42"-long) black inner border strip in half to make 2 (21"-long) pieces. To make each side border, sew a half strip to each full-length strip. Measure length of quilt. Trim borders to size (approximately 45³/₄"). Join borders to quilt sides. Press seam allowances toward borders.
4. Measure width of quilt, including borders, and trim 2 remaining black borders to size (approximately 36¹/₂"). Join borders to quilt top and bottom. Press seam allowances toward borders.

Pieced Border Assembly

1. Select 8 medium/dark fabrics left over from strips (each should be about 24" long). Cut these pieces into 16 (1¹/₄" x 22") strips. Cut the 2 reserved 42"-long light strips in half lengthwise and crosswise to make 8 (1¹/₄" x 22") strips.

Remember to adjust the lengths of your borders if the size of your quilt top differs from the approximate border lengths above. —Liz

2. Referring to Strip Set diagram, join 2¹/₂"-wide and 1¹/₄"-wide strips randomly to make 8 strip sets, approximately 6¹/₂" x 22".   Press seam allowances to 1 side.
3. Cut each strip set into 4 (4¹/₂"-wide) segments.

Strip Set Diagram

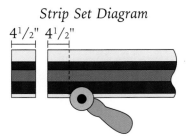

4. Join segments to make 2 (36¹/₂"-long) borders for top and bottom and 2 (47³/₄"-long) side borders. Trim 4 segments to 4¹/₂" squares for border corners.
5. Join 47³/₄"-long borders to quilt sides. Referring to *Quilt Top Assembly Diagram,* page 79, add 1 border corner to both ends of top and bottom borders. Turn border corner squares as shown. Add borders to top and bottom of quilt.

Quilting and Finishing

1. Divide backing fabric into 2 (1¹/₂"-yard) lengths. Join lengthwise to form backing. Border seam will run parallel to quilt top and bottom.
2. Layer backing, batting, and quilt top; baste. Quilt as desired. Quilt shown was utility-quilted (long hand-quilted stitches) with size #8 pearl cotton.
3. Join 2¹/₂"-wide binding strips into 1 continuous piece for straight-grain French-fold binding. Follow *Binding,* page 110, to add binding to quilt.

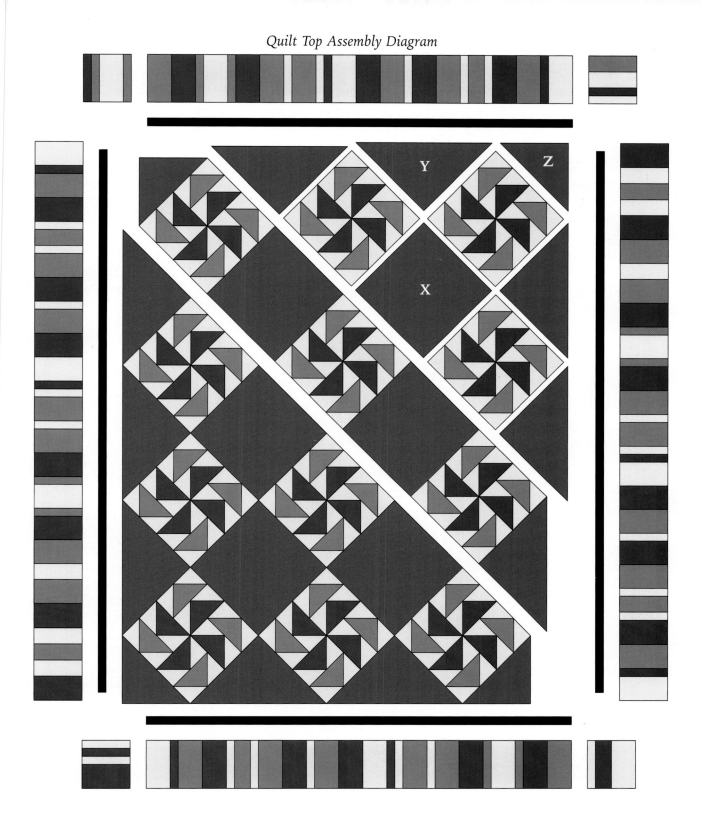

Baby Basket

QUILT BY LIZ PORTER

Finished Size: 42" x 53½" (107 x 136 cm)
Blocks: 18 - 8" (20 cm) Basket Blocks

F eaturing a rainbow of cheerful plaid and striped scraps, this sweet basket quilt is a delightful gift for a newborn. The versatile block is also ideal for a little girl's room; or, add more blocks to make a full-size springtime bed quilt.

Materials

18 - 6" x 12" (15 x 30 cm) scraps of bright
  plaids and stripes for baskets
$1^3/_8$ yards (1.3 m) white print for background
1 yard (91 cm) pink print for setting triangles
  and binding
$^3/_4$ yard (69 cm) pink stripe for borders
$1^5/_8$ yards (1.5 m) fabric for backing
Crib size batting

Cutting

Measurements include $^1/_4$" seam allowance. Cut crosswise strips unless otherwise noted. Follow *Rotary Cutting*, page 100.

From each bright plaid and stripe, cut:
- 1 ($2^7/_8$") square. Cut square in half diagonally to make 2 E half-square triangles for basket bases.
- 4 ($2^1/_2$") squares for diagonal corners C.
- 2 ($2^1/_2$") A squares for basket centers.

From white print, cut:
- 2 ($4^7/_8$"-wide) strips. Cut strips into 9 ($4^7/_8$") squares. Cut squares in half diagonally to make 18 D half-square triangles.
- 1 ($4^1/_2$"-wide) strip. Cut strip into 4 ($4^1/_2$") squares for border corners.
- 12 ($2^1/_2$"-wide) strips. Cut strips into 72 ($2^1/_2$" x $4^1/_2$") B rectangles and 54 ($2^1/_2$") A squares.

From pink print, cut:
- 5 ($2^1/_4$"-wide) strips for binding.
- 1 ($12^5/_8$"-wide) strip. Cut strip into 3 ($12^5/_8$") squares. Cut squares in quarters diagonally to make 10 quarter-square setting triangles. You will have 2 extra.
- 1 ($6^5/_8$") strip. Cut strip into 2 ($6^5/_8$") squares. Cut squares in half diagonally to make 4 half-square corner triangles.

From pink stripe, cut:
- 5 ($4^1/_2$"-wide) strips for borders.

Block Assembly

1. From white print, select 3 A squares, 4 B rectangles, and 1 D triangle. Match these with 1 set of bright scrap pieces (2 As, 4 Cs, and 2 Es).
2. Referring to *Diagonal Seams Diagrams*, lay 1 C square atop left end of 1 B. Stitch diagonally, trim, and press. Repeat at other end. Make 2 of these units.

Diagonal Seams Diagrams

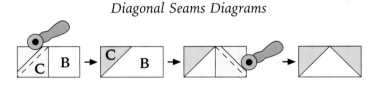

3. Join 2 pairs of contrasting A squares as shown in *Diagram 1*. Press seam allowances toward dark fabric. Join pairs to complete center Four-Patch unit as shown.

Diagram 1

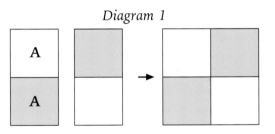

4. Join E triangles to 1 end of each B rectangle as shown in *Diagram 2*. Press seam allowances toward Es.

Diagram 2

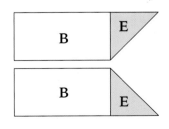

81

5. Lay out pieces as shown in *Block Assembly Diagram*. Join pieces to complete block (*Block Diagram*). Make 18 blocks.

Block Assembly Diagram

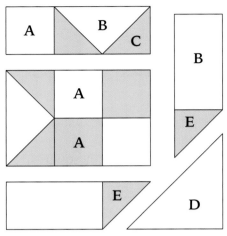

Block Diagram

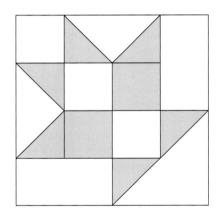

Quilt Assembly

1. Referring to *Quilt Top Assembly Diagram*, page 83, lay out blocks and setting triangles in 6 diagonal rows as shown. Arrange blocks as desired to achieve a pleasing balance of color and value.
2. Join blocks and triangles into diagonal rows. Join rows.
3. Measure length of quilt center. Trim 2 borders to size for quilt sides. Piece borders if necessary. Measure width of quilt, including side borders. Trim 2 borders to size for quilt top and bottom.
4. Add side borders to quilt top. Press seam allowance toward borders.
5. Join corner squares to ends of remaining borders. Join borders to quilt top and bottom.

Quilting and Finishing

1. Layer backing, batting, and quilt top; baste. Quilt as desired. Quilt shown has in-the-ditch quilting with quilting lines extending into setting triangles to form cross-hatching. Liz used a commercial stencil to mark a double-heart motif in border.
2. Join $2^{1}/_{4}$"-wide pink strips into 1 continuous piece for straight-grain French-fold binding. Follow *Binding*, page 110, to add binding to quilt.

Trace, scan, or photocopy this quilt label to finish your quilt.

Katie's Snail's Trail

DESIGNED AND PIECED BY KATIE PORTER; QUILTED BY LYNN WITZENBURG

Finished Size: 72" x 96" (183 x 244 cm)
Blocks: 35 - 12" (30 cm) Snail's Trail Blocks

iz Porter's daughter Katie challenged herself to make a new quilt that looked like an antique. She chose simple fabrics with white patterns in old-time colors for the darks. She gave added interest to the light areas by using lots of shirting prints, plaids, and even pink. Allover Baptist Fan quilting enhanced the antique effect.

Materials

¹/₂ yard (46 cm) each 3 assorted red prints
¹/₂ yard (46 cm) each 5 assorted black prints
¹/₂ yard (46 cm) each 4 assorted blue prints
¹/₂ yard (46 cm) each 3 assorted green prints
¹/₂ yard (46 cm) each 12 assorted light prints
³/₄ yard (69 cm) burgundy print for binding
6 yards (5.5 m) backing
Queen-size batting

Cutting

Measurements include ¹/₄" seam allowances. Cut crosswise strips unless otherwise noted. Follow *Rotary Cutting,* page 100.
Cut sets of matching pieces for blocks as follows: 9 red sets, 10 black sets, 9 blue sets, 7 green sets, and 35 light sets. For each set, cut:
• 1 (6⁷/₈") square. Cut square in half diagonally to make 2 half-square triangles (D).
• 1 (5¹/₈") square. Cut square in half diagonally to make 2 half-square triangles (C).
• 1 (3⁷/₈") square. Cut square in half diagonally to make 2 half-square triangles (B).
• 2 (2⁵/₈") squares (A).
For borders, cut:
• 13 (6⁷/₈") squares from assorted dark prints. Cut squares in half diagonally to make 26 Ds.
• 39 (6⁷/₈") squares from assorted light prints. Cut squares in half diagonally to make 78 Ds.
From burgundy print, cut:
• 9 (2¹/₄"-wide) strips for binding.

Block Assembly

1. Choose 1 light and 1 dark block set. Join 1 dark A to 1 light A. Repeat. Referring to *Four-Patch Diagram,* join units to make a Four-Patch unit.

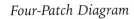

Four-Patch Diagram

2. Referring to *Block Assembly Diagram,* join 2 light and 2 dark Bs to opposite sides of Four-Patch unit. Continue with Cs and Ds. Be sure to follow diagram exactly so that block will swirl in proper direction.

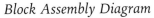

Block Assembly Diagram

3. Make 35 Snail's Trail blocks: 9 red, 10 black, 9 blue, and 7 green (*Block Diagram*).

Block Diagram

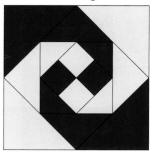

Quilt Assembly

1. Referring to *Quilt Top Assembly Diagram,* page 87, arrange blocks in 7 horizontal rows of 5 blocks each, rotating blocks as shown. Be sure that each large square formed by the dark Ds has 1 triangle of each color in it. Join blocks into rows; join rows to complete center.
2. Referring to *Border Unit Diagram,* join l light D and 1 dark D to make a light/dark border unit. Make 26 light/dark border units.

Border Unit Diagram

3. Join 2 light Ds to make a light border unit. Make 26 light border units.
4. Referring to *Quilt Top Assembly Diagram,* lay out 14 border units each to make 2 side borders. Make sure that each large square formed by dark Ds has 1 triangle of each color in it. Join units. Add borders to quilt sides. Join 12 border units in same manner to make top and bottom borders. Add borders to quilt.

Quilting and Finishing

1. Divide backing fabric into 2 (3-yard) lengths. Cut 1 piece in half lengthwise. Sew 1 narrow panel to each side of wide panel. Press seam allowances toward narrow panels.
2. Layer backing, batting, and quilt top; baste. Quilt as desired. Quilt shown was machine-quilted in Baptist Fans. See *Baptist Fan Quilting,* page 88.
3. Join 2^1/$_4$"-wide burgundy strips into 1 continuous piece for straight-grain French-fold binding. Follow *Binding,* page 110, to add binding to quilt.

Baptist Fan Quilting

By Liz Porter

The Baptist Fan has been a popular quilting design for more than 100 years. The concentric arcs of the design are easy to quilt and are a pleasing complement to the sharp angles of most patchwork patterns.

Materials
9" x 12" sheet of template plastic
Household scissors

Traditionally, the Baptist Fan design was marked using a dinner plate or a makeshift compass made by typing a length of string around a pencil. Knots were spaced at 1" intervals along the string to determine the center point of the arc from which to swing the compass. Marking was not always accurate, due to the "play" in the string. Quilters today usually demand more accuracy than is possible with the string method.

Although there are now commercial quilting stencils available to mark this design, I find them difficult to use and prefer my homemade version. To make your own stencil for Baptist Fan and to use it to mark your quilt, follow these simple steps:

1. Place a sheet of template plastic over the pattern on pages 90 – 91 and trace. Cut around outside of the stencil. Then cut out the shaded areas, leaving bridges to hold the stencil together.

2. To mark the design on your quilt, begin at the lower right corner of your quilt and use the stencil to mark the arcs as shown in *photo A*. The right edge of your stencil will line up with the right edge of your quilt top. The lower part of the stencil will hang below the bottom edge of your quilt top.

3. Mark a second set of eight arcs along the bottom edge of the quilt top, pivoting your stencil from the point where the largest arc in the first set met the bottom edge of the quilt top (*photo B*). Pivot the stencil to mark the top arcs so that they meet the first set (*photo C*). In a similar manner, mark the entire first row of arcs along the bottom edges of the quilt top.

4. To mark the next row of arcs, again begin at the right edge of the quilt top (*photo D*). Mark successive arcs from right to left and pivot the stencil as needed to complete the arcs (*photo E*). Continue to mark arcs in rows until the entire quilt top is marked.

The pattern name refers to the cardboard fans used in the summertime in country churches. —Liz and Marianne

A

B

C

D

E

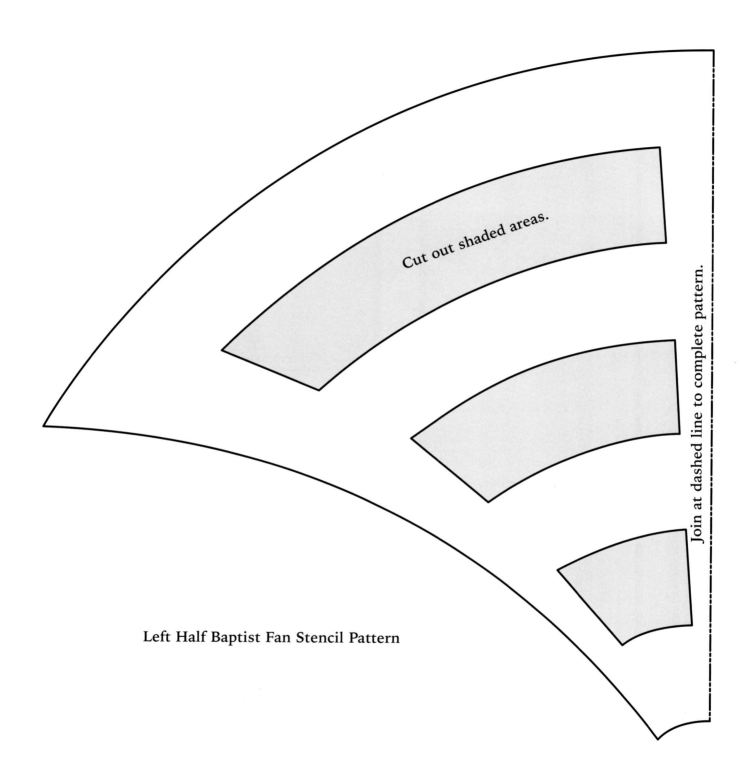

Cut out shaded areas.

Join at dashed line to complete pattern.

Left Half Baptist Fan Stencil Pattern

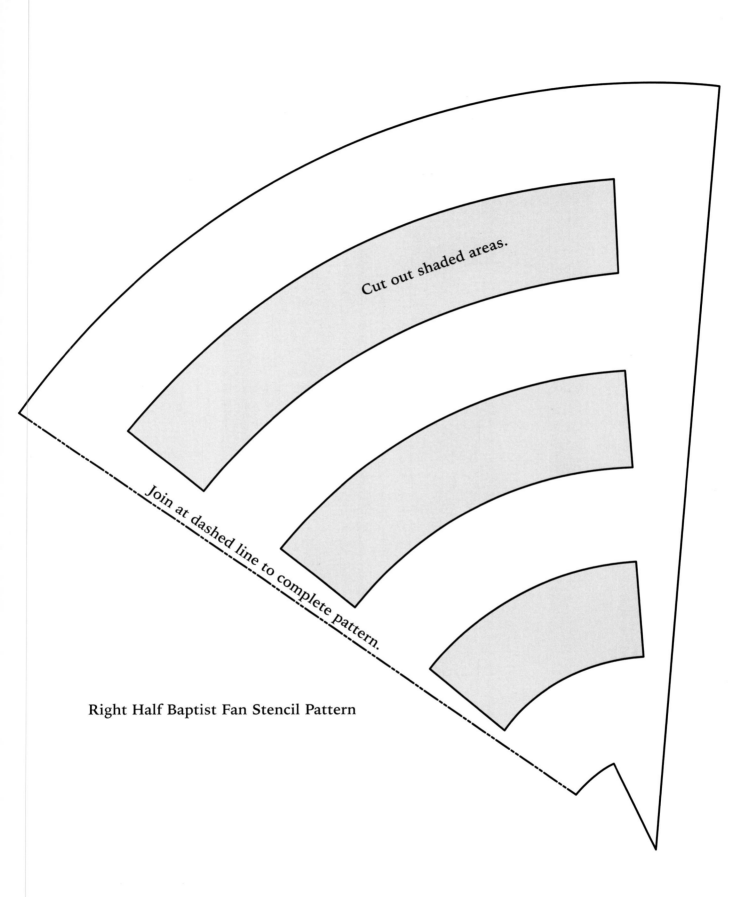

Cut out shaded areas.

Join at dashed line to complete pattern.

Right Half Baptist Fan Stencil Pattern

Floating Plaids

QUILT DESIGNED AND MADE BY CONNIE AYERS

Finished Size: 35" x 49" (89 x 124 cm)
Blocks: 6 - 11" (28 cm) blocks

"This quilt started out as a traditional plaid scrap quilt," says Connie Ayers. "Inspired by a television program on physics, I painted a design onto fabric with a small brush, drawing what I envision anti-matter to look like. The motif gave the whole quilt a more contemporary look." Instead of painting your own fabric, try a zippy batik print for your sashing and borders.

Materials

12 fat eighths* assorted dark stripes and plaids for strip sets
4 fat eights* dark plaids for stars
4 fat eights* assorted light prints for star backgrounds
3/4 yard (69 cm) red batik print for border and sashing
3/4 yard (69 cm) black print for border and binding
1 1/2 yards (1.4 m) fabric for backing
Crib-size batting
*Fat eighth = 9" x 22"

Cutting

Measurements include 1/4" seam allowances. Cut crosswise strips unless otherwise noted. Border strips are exact length needed. You may want to cut them longer to allow for piecing variations. Position all rectangles *right side up* before making diagonal cuts to divide them into triangles. Follow *Rotary Cutting,* page 100.

From assorted dark stripe and plaid fat eighths, cut:
- 4 (3"-wide) strips (I).
- 4 (2 1/4"-wide) strips (J).
- 4 (1 3/4"-wide) strips (K).
- 4 sets of 6 (1 3/4" x 2 1/4") rectangles (B).

From each dark plaid fat eighth, cut:
- 6 (1 5/8" x 3") rectangles. Cut rectangles in half diagonally, from lower right to upper left, to make 12 As.
- 3 (2" x 3 3/4") rectangles. Cut rectangles in half diagonally, from lower right to upper left, to make 6 Cs.
- 3 (1 1/2" x 4 1/4") rectangles. Cut rectangles in half diagonally, from lower right to upper left, to make 6 Ds.
- 3 (2 1/8") squares. Cut squares in half diagonally to make 6 Gs.
- 3 (1 5/8" x 2 3/8") rectangles. Cut rectangles in half diagonally, from lower right to upper left, to make 6 Hs.

From each light fat eighth, cut:
- 6 (1 5/8" x 3") rectangles. Cut rectangles in half diagonally, from lower right to upper left, to make 12 As.
- 3 (2" x 3 3/4") rectangles. Cut rectangles in half diagonally, from lower right to upper left, to make 6 Cs.
- 3 (1 1/2" x 4 1/4") rectangles. Cut rectangles in half diagonally, from lower right to upper left, to make 6 Ds.
- 6 (1 3/8" x 3") rectangles (E).
- 6 (1 3/8" x 1 3/4") rectangles (F).
- 3 (2 1/8") squares. Cut squares in half diagonally to make 6 Gs.
- 3 (1 5/8" x 2 3/8") rectangles. Cut rectangles in half diagonally, from lower right to upper left, to make 6 Hs.

From red batik print, cut:
- 7 (3 1/2"-wide) strips. Cut strips into:
  - 2 (3 1/2" x 39 1/2") side borders.
  - 2 (3 1/2" x 31 1/2") top and bottom borders.
  - 1 (3 1/2" x 39 1/2") center sashing strip.
  - 4 (3 1/2" x 11 1/2") horizontal sashing strips.

From black print, cut:
- 5 (2 1/2"-wide) strips. Piece to make:
  - 2 (2 1/2" x 45 1/2") side borders.
  - 2 (3 1/2" x 35 1/2") top and bottom borders.
- 5 (2 1/4"-wide) strips for binding.

Block Assembly

1. Referring to *Strip Set Diagram*, join 1 of each of the following along long sides to make 1 strip set: 1 (3"-wide) I, 1 (2¼"-wide) J, and 1 (1¾"-wide) K. Press seams in same direction. Make 4 assorted strip sets.

Strip Set Diagram

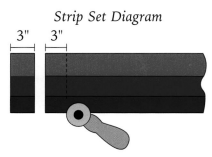

2. Cut each strip set into 6 (3"-wide) side strips.
3. Separate star pieces into star groups. You will need 6 matching sets in each of 4 fabric combinations, consisting of matching lights (2As, 1 C, 1 D, 1 E, 1 F, 1 G, 1 H), matching darks (2 As, 1 C, 1 D, 1 G, 1 H), and 1 contrasting dark B.
4. Referring to *Unit Assembly Diagram*, join 1 dark and 1 light D to make a half-rectangle unit. (See opposite page for basic half-rectangle unit instructions.) Join 1 dark and 1 light C. Join with 1 light E and D unit as shown to complete Row 1.

Unit Assembly Diagram

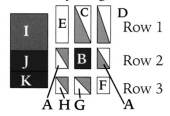

5. Join 1 dark A and 1 light A to make a half-rectangle unit. Repeat. Join A units to each side of 1 B as shown to complete Row 2.
6. Join 1 dark and 1 light G. Join 1 dark and 1 light H. Join with 1 light F as shown to complete Row 3.
7. Join Rows 1-3 as shown to complete 1 star unit. Join 1 side strip to left side of star (*Unit Diagram*).

Unit Diagram

8. Repeat Steps 4-7 to make 6 matching units, 1 for each block. Make 4 sets of 6 units.
9. Lay out units in 6 matching blocks as shown in *Block Assembly Diagram*. Join to complete blocks (*Block Diagram*).

Block Assembly Diagram

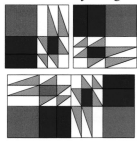
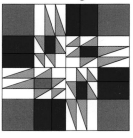

Block Diagram

Try This!

Pattern tester Pat Myers went for a more subdued look in her block. However, she was still able to incorporate a marbled fabric for emphasis. Instead of using it in the borders, she put it in the center of each rectangle star and in the block corners. Then she framed the block with a tone-on-tone blue print.

94

Quilt Assembly

1. Lay out blocks and horizontal sashing strips as shown in *Quilt Top Assembly Diagram*. Join to make vertical rows. Join rows with vertical sashing.
2. Add side red batik borders to quilt. Press seam allowances toward borders. Add remaining 2 red borders to top and bottom of quilt.
3. Add black borders to quilt as in Step 2.

Quilting and Finishing

1. Layer backing, batting, and quilt top; baste. Quilt as desired. Quilt shown was quilted in wavy parallel rows.
2. Join 2¼"-wide black print strips into 1 continuous piece for straight-grain French-fold binding. Follow *Binding*, page 110, to add binding to quilt.

Quilt Top Assembly Diagram

Working with
Half-Rectangle Triangles

You're probably used to working with half-square triangles in your quilts. Half-rectangles go together differently. Follow the directions below, and your blocks will finish correctly.

1. In order to see what happens to your $1/4$" seam allowance, use a ruler to draw a sewing line $1/4$" all around the wrong side of your half-rectangle pieces, as shown in *Diagram 1*.

2. See how far the point of fabric extends beyond the sewing line you just drew? It is much longer than $1/4$". If you try to align the raw edges when you join the two triangles together, the seam lines will not be aligned. Instead, you must pin-match the 2 pieces at the $1/4$" seam lines intersection, which looks like an elongated X (circled in red in *Diagram 2*) before stitching them together.

3. If you pin and sew the pieces together accurately, the lines you drew will match, and you will have a long, skinny tail at each end, as shown in *Diagram 3*.

4. Trim the excess tails and seam allowances even with the sides of the rectangle unit. At this stage, the diagonal seam will not split the unit exactly in half (*Diagram 4*). Don't worry–this is the way it should look. When these rectangle units are joined to other pieces with $1/4$" seams, the diagonal split will be at the corners.

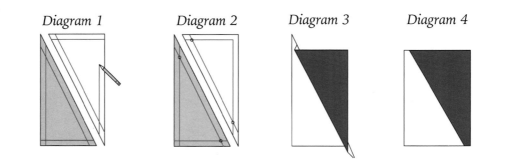

| *Diagram 1* | *Diagram 2* | *Diagram 3* | *Diagram 4* |

General Instructions

Complete instructions are given for making each of the quilts shown in this book. To make your quilting easier and more enjoyable, we encourage you to carefully read all of the general instructions, study the color photographs, and familiarize yourself with the individual project instructions before beginning a project.

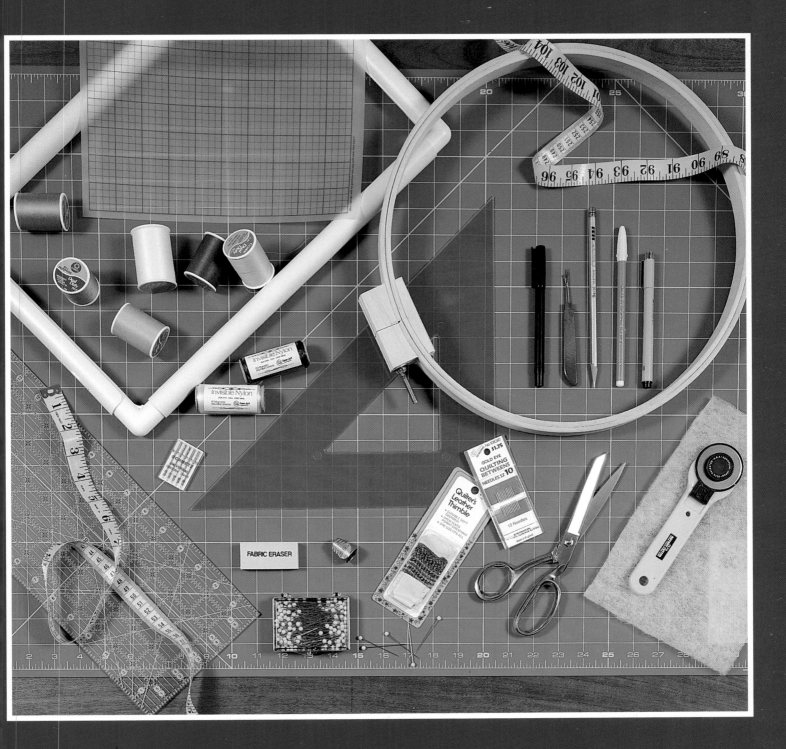

QUILTING SUPPLIES

This list includes all the tools you need for basic quick-method quiltmaking, plus additional supplies used for special techniques. Unless otherwise specified, all items may be found in your favorite fabric store or quilt shop.

Batting — Batting is most commonly available in polyester, cotton, or a polyester/cotton blend (see **Choosing and Preparing the Batting**, page 107).

Cutting mat — A cutting mat is a special mat designed to be used with a rotary cutter. A mat that measures approximately 18" x 24" is a good size for most cutting.

Eraser — A soft white fabric eraser or white art eraser may be used to remove pencil marks from fabric. Do not use a colored eraser, as the dye may discolor fabric.

Iron — An iron with both steam and dry settings and a smooth, clean soleplate is necessary for proper pressing.

Marking tools — There are many different marking tools available (see **Marking Quilting Lines**, page 106). A silver quilter's pencil is a good marker for both light and dark fabrics.

Masking tape — Two widths of masking tape, 1"-wide and 1/4"-wide, are helpful when quilting. The 1"-wide tape is used to secure the backing fabric to a flat surface when layering the quilt. The 1/4"-wide tape may be used as a guide when outline quilting.

Needles — Two types of needles are used for hand sewing: Betweens, used for quilting, are short and strong for stitching through layered fabric and batting. Sharps are longer, thinner needles used for basting and other hand sewing. For sewing machine needles, we recommend size 10 to 14 or 70 to 90 universal (sharp-pointed) needles.

Permanent fine-point pen — A permanent pen is used to mark templates and stencils and to sign and date quilts. Test pen on fabric to make sure it will not bleed or wash out.

Pins — Straight pins made especially for quilting are extra long with large round heads. Glass head pins will stand up to occasional contact with a hot iron. Some quilters prefer extra-fine dressmaker's silk pins. If you are machine quilting, you will need a large supply of 1" long (size 01) rustproof safety pins for pin-basting.

Quilting hoop or frame — Quilting hoops and frames are designed to hold the 3 layers of a quilt together securely while you quilt. Many different types and sizes are available, including round and oval wooden hoops, frames made of rigid plastic pipe, and large floor frames made of either material. A 14" or 16" hoop allows you to quilt in your lap and makes your quilting portable.

Rotary cutter — The rotary cutter is the essential tool for quick-method quilting techniques. The cutter consists of a round, sharp blade mounted on a handle with a retractable blade guard for safety. It should be used only with a cutting mat and rotary cutting ruler. Three sizes are generally available; we recommend the 45 mm size.

Rotary cutting ruler — A rotary cutting ruler is a thick, clear acrylic ruler made specifically for use with a rotary cutter. It should have accurate 1/8" crosswise and lengthwise markings and markings for 45° and 60° angles. A 6" x 24" ruler is a good size for most cutting. An additional 6" x 12" ruler or 12 1/2" square ruler is helpful when cutting wider pieces. Many specialty rulers are available that make specific cutting tasks faster and easier.

Scissors — Although most fabric cutting will be done with a rotary cutter, sharp, high-quality scissors are still needed for some cutting. A separate pair of scissors for cutting paper and plastic is recommended. Smaller scissors are handy for clipping threads.

Seam ripper — A good seam ripper with a fine point is useful for removing stitching.

Sewing machine — A sewing machine that produces a good, even straight stitch is all that is necessary for most quilting. Clean and oil your machine often and keep the tension set properly.

Tape measure — A flexible 120" long tape measure is helpful for measuring a quilt top before adding borders.

Template material — Sheets of translucent plastic, often pre-marked with a grid, are made especially for making quilting stencils.

Thimble — A thimble is necessary when hand quilting. Thimbles are available in metal, plastic, or leather and in many sizes and styles. Choose a thimble that fits well and is comfortable.

Thread — Several types of thread are used for quiltmaking: *General-purpose* sewing thread is used for basting and piecing. Choose high-quality cotton or cotton-covered polyester thread in light and dark neutrals, such as ecru and grey, for your basic supplies. *Quilting* thread is stronger than general-purpose sewing thread, and some brands have a coating to make them slide more easily through the quilt layers.

Triangle — A large plastic right-angle triangle (available in art and office supply stores) is useful in rotary cutting for making first cuts to "square up" raw edges of fabric and for checking to see that cuts remain at right angles to the fold.

Walking foot — A walking foot, or even-feed foot, is needed for straight-line machine quilting. This special foot will help all 3 layers move at the same rate over the feed dogs to provide a smoother quilted project.

FABRICS

SELECTING FABRICS

Choose high-quality, medium-weight 100% cotton fabrics such as broadcloth or calico. All-cotton fabrics hold a crease better, fray less, and are easier to quilt than cotton/polyester blends. All the fabrics for a quilt should be of comparable weight and weave. Check the end of the fabric bolt for fiber content and width.

The yardage requirements listed for each project are based on 45" wide fabric with a "usable" width of 42" after shrinkage and trimming selvages. Your actual usable width will probably vary slightly from fabric to fabric. Though most fabrics will yield 42" or more, if you find a fabric that you suspect will yield a narrower usable width, you will need to purchase additional yardage to compensate. Our recommended yardage lengths should be adequate for occasional resquaring of fabric when many cuts are required, but it never hurts to buy a little more fabric for insurance against a narrower usable width, the occasional cutting error, or to have on hand for making coordinating projects.

PREPARING FABRICS

All fabrics should be washed, dried, and pressed before cutting.

1. To check colorfastness before washing, cut a small piece of the fabric and place in a glass of hot water with a little detergent. Leave fabric in the water for a few minutes. Remove fabric from water and blot with white paper towels. If any color bleeds onto the towels, wash the fabric separately with warm water and detergent, then rinse until the water runs clear. If fabric continues to bleed, choose another fabric.

2. Unfold yardage and separate fabrics by color. To help reduce raveling, use scissors to snip a small triangle from each corner of your fabric pieces. Machine wash fabrics in warm water with a small amount of mild laundry detergent. Do not use fabric softener. Rinse well and then dry fabrics in the dryer, checking long fabric lengths occasionally to make sure they are not tangling.

3. To make ironing easier, remove fabrics from dryer while they are slightly damp. Refold each fabric lengthwise (as it was on the bolt) with wrong sides together and matching selvages. If necessary, adjust slightly at selvages so that fold lays flat. Press each fabric using a steam iron set on "cotton."

ROTARY CUTTING

*Based on the idea that you can easily cut strips of fabric and then cut those strips into smaller pieces, rotary cutting has brought speed and accuracy to quiltmaking. Observe safety precautions when using the rotary cutter, since it is extremely sharp. Develop a habit of retracting the blade guard **just before** making a cut and closing it **immediately afterward**, before laying down the cutter.*

1. Follow **Preparing Fabrics**, page 99, to wash, dry, and press fabrics.

2. Cut all strips from the selvage-to-selvage width of the fabric unless otherwise indicated in project instructions. Place fabric on the cutting mat, as shown in *Fig. 1*, with the fold of the fabric toward you. To straighten the uneven fabric edge, make the first "squaring up" cut by placing the right edge of the rotary cutting ruler over the left raw edge of the fabric. Place right-angle triangle (or another rotary cutting ruler) with the lower edge carefully aligned with the fold and the left edge against the ruler (*Fig. 1*). Hold the ruler firmly with your left hand, placing your little finger off the left edge to anchor the ruler. Remove the triangle, pick up the rotary cutter, and retract the blade guard. Using a smooth downward motion, make the cut by running the blade of the rotary cutter firmly along the right edge of the ruler (*Fig. 2*). **Always** cut in a direction **away** from your body and **immediately** close the blade guard after each cut.

Fig. 1

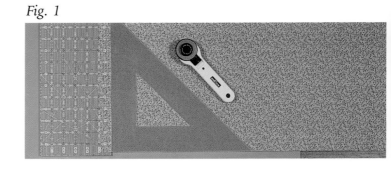

Fig. 2

3. To cut each of the strips required for a project, place the ruler over the cut edge of the fabric, aligning desired marking on the ruler with the cut edge (*Fig. 3*); make the cut. When cutting several strips from a single piece of fabric, it is important to occasionally use the ruler and triangle to ensure that cuts are still at a perfect right angle to the fold. If not, repeat Step 2 to straighten.

Fig. 3

4. To square up selvage ends of a strip before cutting pieces, refer to *Fig. 4* and place folded strip on mat with selvage ends to your right. Aligning a horizontal marking on ruler with 1 long edge of strip, use rotary cutter to trim selvage to make end of strip square and even *(Fig. 4)*. Turn strip (or entire mat) so that cut end is to your left before making subsequent cuts.

Fig. 4

5. Pieces such as rectangles and squares can now be cut from strips. Usually strips remain folded, and pieces are cut in pairs after ends of strips are squared up. To cut squares or rectangles from a strip, place ruler over left end of strip, aligning desired marking on ruler with cut end of strip. To ensure perfectly square cuts, align a horizontal marking on ruler with 1 long edge of strip *(Fig. 5)* before making the cut.

Fig. 5

6. To cut 2 triangles from a square, cut square the size indicated in the project instructions. Cut square once diagonally to make 2 triangles *(Fig. 6)*.

Fig. 6

7. To cut 4 triangles from a square, cut square the size indicated in the project instructions. Cut square twice diagonally to make 4 triangles *(Fig. 7)*. You may find it helpful to use a small rotary cutting mat so that the mat can be turned to make second cut without disturbing fabric pieces.

Fig. 7

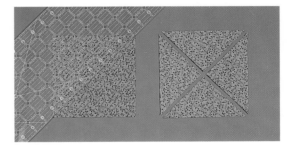

8. After some practice, you may want to try stacking up to 6 fabric layers when making cuts. When stacking strips, match long cut edges and follow Step 4 to square up ends of strip stack. Carefully turn stack (or entire mat) so that squared-up ends are to your left before making subsequent cuts. After cutting, check accuracy of pieces. Some shapes, such as diamonds, are more difficult to cut accurately in stacks.

9. In some cases, strips will be sewn together into strip sets before being cut into smaller units. When cutting a strip set, align a seam in strip set with a horizontal marking on the ruler to maintain square cuts *(Fig. 8)*. We do not recommend stacking strip sets for rotary cutting.

Fig. 8

PIECING AND PRESSING

Precise cutting, followed by accurate piecing and careful pressing, will ensure that all the pieces of your quilt top fit together well.

PIECING

Set sewing machine stitch length for approximately 11 stitches per inch. Use a new, sharp needle suited for medium-weight woven fabric.

Use a neutral-colored general-purpose sewing thread (not quilting thread) in the needle and in the bobbin. Stitch first on a scrap of fabric to check upper and bobbin thread tension; make any adjustments necessary.

For good results, it is **essential** that you stitch with an **accurate** ¹⁄₄" **seam allowance**. On many sewing machines, the measurement from the needle to the outer edge of the presser foot is ¹⁄₄". If this is the case with your machine, the presser foot is your best guide. If not, measure ¹⁄₄" from the needle and mark throat plate with a piece of masking tape. Special presser feet that are exactly ¹⁄₄" wide are also available for most sewing machines.

When piecing, **always** place pieces **right sides together** and **match raw edges**; pin if necessary. (If using straight pins, remove the pins just before they reach the sewing machine needle.)

Chain Piecing

Chain piecing whenever possible will make your work go faster and will usually result in more accurate piecing. Stack the pieces you will be sewing beside your machine in the order you will need them and in a position that will allow you to easily pick them up. Pick up each pair of pieces, carefully place them together as they will be sewn, and feed them into the machine one after the other. Stop between each pair only long enough to pick up the next pair; don't cut thread between pairs *(Fig. 9)*. After all pieces are sewn, cut threads, press, and go on to the next step, chain piecing when possible.

Fig. 9

Sewing Strip Sets

When there are several strips to assemble into a strip set, first sew the strips together into pairs, then sew the pairs together to form the strip set. To help avoid distortion, sew 1 seam in 1 direction and then sew the next seam in the opposite direction (*Fig. 10*).

Fig. 10

Sewing Across Seam Intersections

When sewing across the intersection of 2 seams, place pieces right sides together and match seams exactly, making sure seam allowances are pressed in opposite directions (*Fig. 11*). To prevent fabric from shifting, you may wish to pin in place.

Fig. 11

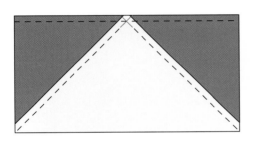

Sewing Bias Seams

Care should be used in handling and stitching bias edges since they stretch easily. After sewing the seam, carefully press seam allowance to 1 side, making sure not to stretch fabric.

Sewing Sharp Points

To ensure sharp points when joining triangular or diagonal pieces, stitch across the center of the "X" (shown in pink) formed on the wrong side by previous seams (*Fig. 12*).

Fig. 12

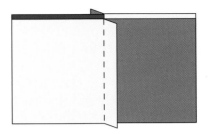

Trimming Seam Allowances

When sewing with triangle pieces, some seam allowances may extend beyond the edges of the sewn pieces. Trim away "dog ears" that extend beyond the edges of the sewn pieces (*Fig. 13*).

Fig. 13

Pressing

Use a steam iron set on "cotton" for all pressing. Press as you sew, taking care to prevent small folds along seamlines. Seam allowances are almost always pressed to one side, usually toward the darker fabric. However, to reduce bulk it may occasionally be necessary to press seam allowances toward the lighter fabric or even to press them open. In order to prevent a dark fabric seam allowance from showing through a light fabric, trim the darker seam allowance slightly narrower than the lighter seam allowance. To press long seams, such as those in long strip sets, without curving or other distortion, lay strips across the width of the ironing board.

APPLIQUÉ

SATIN STITCH APPLIQUÉING

A good satin stitch is a thick, smooth, almost solid line of zigzag stitching that covers the exposed raw edges of appliqué pieces.

1. Place a stabilizer, such as paper or any of the commercially available products, on wrong side of background fabric before stitching appliqués in place.

2. Thread needle of sewing machine with general-purpose thread. Use thread that matches the background fabric in the bobbin for all stitching. Set sewing machine for a medium width zigzag stitch (approximately $^1/_8$") and a very short stitch length. Set upper tension slightly looser than for regular stitching.

3. Beginning on as straight an edge as possible, position fabric so that most of the satin stitch will be on the appliqué piece. Do not backstitch; hold upper thread toward you and sew over it two or three stitches to anchor thread. Following Steps 4–7 for stitching corners and curves, stitch over exposed raw edges of appliqué pieces, changing thread color as necessary.

4. *(Note: Dots on Figs. indicate where to leave needle in fabric when pivoting.)* For outside corners, stitch $^1/_8$" past the corner, stopping with the needle in background fabric *(Fig. 14)*. Raise presser foot. Pivot project, lower presser foot, and stitch adjacent side *(Fig. 15)*.

Fig. 14

Fig. 15

5. For inside corners, stitch $^1/_8$" past the corner, stopping with the needle in the appliqué fabric *(Fig. 16)*. Raise presser foot. Pivot project, lower presser foot, and stitch adjacent side *(Fig. 17)*.

Fig. 16   *Fig. 17*

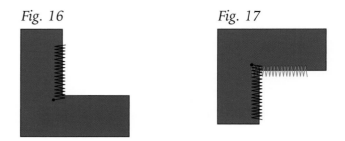

6. When stitching outside curves, stop with needle in background fabric. Raise presser foot and pivot project as needed. Lower presser foot and continue stitching, pivoting as often as necessary to follow curve *(Fig. 18)*. When stitching inside curves, stop with needle in appliqué fabric. Raise presser foot and pivot project as needed. Lower presser foot and continue stitching, pivoting as often as necessary to follow curve *(Fig. 19)*.

Fig. 18   *Fig. 19*

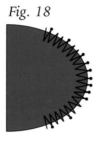

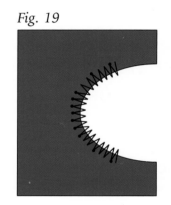

7. Do not backstitch at end of stitching. Pull threads to wrong side of background fabric; knot thread and trim ends. Remove paper and stabilizer.

HAND APPLIQUÉ

In this traditional hand appliqué method, the needle is used to turn the seam allowance under as you sew the appliqué to the background fabric using a Blind Stitch.

1. Place template on right side of appliqué fabric. Use a pencil to lightly draw around template, leaving at least 1/2" between shapes; repeat for number of shapes specified in project instructions.
2. Cut out shapes approximately 3/16" outside drawn line. Clip inside curves and points up to, but not through, drawn line. Arrange shapes on background fabric and pin or baste in place.
3. Thread a sharps needle with a single strand of general purpose sewing thread; knot one end.
4. For each appliqué shape, begin on as straight an edge as possible and turn a small section of seam allowance to wrong side with needle, concealing drawn line. Use Blind Stitch to sew appliqué to background, turning under edge and stitching as you continue around shape. Do not turn under or stitch seam allowances that will be covered by other appliqué pieces.
5. Follow **Cutting Away Fabric From Behind Appliqués** to reduce bulk behind appliqués.

CUTTING AWAY FABRIC FROM BEHIND APPLIQUÉS

Hand quilting an appliquéd block will be easier if you are stitching through as few layers as possible. For this reason, or just to reduce bulk in your quilt, you may wish to cut away the background fabric behind appliqués. After stitching appliqués in place, turn block over and use sharp scissors or specially-designed appliqué scissors to trim away background fabric approximately 3/16" from stitching line. Take care not to cut appliqué fabric or stitches.

QUILTING

*Quilting holds the 3 layers (top, batting, and backing) of the quilt together and can be done by hand or machine. Our project instructions tell you which method is used on each project and show you quilting diagrams that can be used as suggestions for marking quilting designs. Because marking, layering, and quilting are interrelated and may be done in different orders depending on circumstances, please read the entire **Quilting** section, pages 105 - 109, before beginning the quilting process on your project.*

TYPES OF QUILTING

In-the-Ditch

Quilting along seamlines *(Fig. 20)* or along edges of appliqué *(Fig. 21)* is called "in-the-ditch" quilting. This type of quilting does not need to be marked. When quilting in the ditch, quilt on the side **opposite** the seam allowance.

Fig. 20

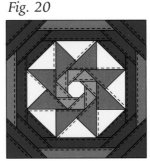

Fig. 21

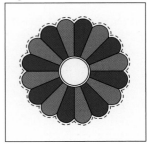

Outline Quilting

Quilting a consistent distance, usually $1/4"$, from a seam or appliqué is called "outline" quilting (Fig. 22). Outline quilting may be marked, or you may place $1/4"$-wide masking tape along seamlines and quilt along the opposite edge of the tape. (Do not leave tape on quilt longer than necessary, since it may leave an adhesive residue.)

Fig. 22

Ornamental Quilting

Quilting decorative lines or designs is called "ornamental" quilting (Fig. 23). This type of quilting should be marked before you baste quilt layers together.

Fig. 23

MARKING QUILTING LINES

Fabric marking pencils, various types of chalk markers, and fabric marking pens with inks that disappear with exposure to air or water are readily available and work well for different applications. Lead pencils work well on light-color fabrics, but marks may be difficult to remove. White pencils work well on dark-color fabrics, and silver pencils show up well on many colors. Since chalk rubs off easily, it's a good choice if you are marking as you quilt. Fabric marking pens make more durable and visible markings, but the marks should be carefully removed according to manufacturer's instructions. Press down only as hard as necessary to make a visible line.

When you choose to mark your quilt, whether before or after the layers are basted together, is also a factor in deciding which marking tool to use. If you mark with chalk or a chalk pencil, handling the quilt during basting may rub off the markings. Intricate or ornamental designs may not be practical to mark as you quilt; mark these designs before basting using a more durable marker.

To choose marking tools, take all these factors into consideration and **test** different markers **on scrap fabric** until you find the one that gives the desired result.

USING QUILTING STENCILS

A wide variety of precut quilting stencils, as well as entire books of quilting patterns, are available. Using a stencil makes it easier to mark intricate or repetitive designs on your quilt top.

1. To make a stencil from a pattern, center template plastic over pattern and use a permanent marker to trace pattern onto plastic.
2. Use a craft knife with a single or double blade to cut narrow slits along traced lines *(Fig. 24)*.

Fig. 24

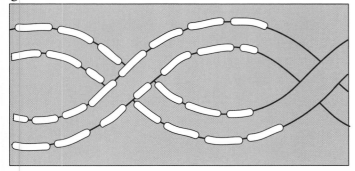

3. Use desired marking tool and stencil to mark quilting lines.

CHOOSING AND PREPARING THE BATTING

Choosing the right batting will make your quilting job easier. For fine hand quilting, choose a low-loft batting in any of the fiber types described here. Machine quilters will want to choose a low-loft batting that is all cotton or a cotton/polyester blend because the cotton helps "grip" the layers of the quilt. If the quilt is to be tied, a high-loft batting, sometimes called extra-loft or fat batting, is a good choice.

Batting is available in many different fibers. Bonded polyester batting is one of the most popular batting types. It is treated with a protective coating to stabilize the fibers and to reduce "bearding," a process in which batting fibers work their way out through the quilt fabrics. Other batting options include cotton/polyester batting, which combines the best of both polyester and cotton battings; all-cotton batting, which must be quilted more closely than polyester batting; and wool and silk battings, which are generally more expensive and usually only dry-cleanable.

Whichever batting you choose, read the manufacturer's instructions closely for any special notes on care or preparation. When you're ready to use your chosen batting in a project, cut batting the same size as the prepared backing.

ASSEMBLING THE QUILT

1. Examine wrong side of quilt top closely; trim any seam allowances and clip any threads that may show through the front of the quilt. Press quilt top.
2. If quilt top is to be marked before layering, mark quilting lines (see **Marking Quilting Lines**, page 106).
3. Place backing **wrong** side up on a flat surface. Use masking tape to tape edges of backing to surface. Place batting on top of backing fabric. Smooth batting gently, being careful not to stretch or tear. Center quilt top **right** side up on batting.
4. If hand quilting, begin in the center and work toward the outer edges to hand baste all layers together. Use long stitches and place basting lines approximately 4" apart *(Fig. 25)*. Smooth fullness or wrinkles toward outer edges.

Fig. 25

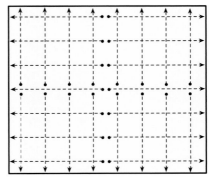

5. If machine quilting, use 1" rustproof safety pins to "pin-baste" all layers together, spacing pins approximately 4" apart. Begin at the center and work toward the outer edges to secure all layers. If possible, place pins away from areas that will be quilted, although pins may be removed as needed when quilting.

HAND QUILTING

The quilting stitch is a basic running stitch that forms a broken line on the quilt top and backing. Stitches on the quilt top and backing should be straight and equal in length.

1. Secure center of quilt in hoop or frame. Check quilt top and backing to make sure they are smooth. To help prevent puckers, always begin quilting in the center of the quilt and work toward the outside edges.

2. Thread needle with an 18" - 20" length of quilting thread; knot 1 end. Using a thimble, insert needle into quilt top and batting approximately $1/2$" from where you wish to begin quilting. Bring needle up at the point where you wish to begin *(Fig. 26)*; when knot catches on quilt top, give thread a quick, short pull to "pop" knot through fabric into batting *(Fig. 27)*.

3. Holding the needle with your sewing hand and placing your other hand underneath the quilt, use thimble to push the tip of the needle down through all layers. As soon as needle touches your finger underneath, use that finger to push the tip of the needle only back up through the layers to top of quilt. (The amount of the needle showing above the fabric determines the length of the quilting stitch.) Referring to *Fig. 28*, rock the needle up and down, taking 3 - 6 stitches before bringing the needle and thread completely through the layers. Check the back of the quilt to make sure stitches are going through all layers. When quilting through a seam allowance or quilting a curve or corner, you may need to make 1 stitch at a time.

Fig. 28

4. When you reach the end of your thread, knot thread close to the fabric and "pop" knot into batting; clip thread close to fabric.

5. Stop and move your hoop as often as necessary. You do not have to tie a knot every time you move your hoop; you may leave the thread dangling and pick it up again when you return to that part of the quilt.

Fig. 26

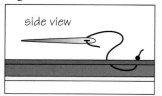

Fig. 27

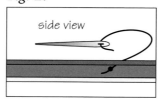

MACHINE QUILTING

The following instructions are for straight-line quilting, which requires a walking foot or even-feed foot. The term "straight-line" is somewhat deceptive, since curves (especially gentle ones) as well as straight lines can be stitched with this technique.

1. Wind your sewing machine bobbin with general-purpose thread that matches the quilt backing. Do not use quilting thread. Thread the needle of your machine with transparent monofilament thread if you want your quilting to blend with your quilt top fabrics. Use decorative thread, such as a metallic or contrasting-color general-purpose thread, when you want the quilting lines to stand out more. Set the stitch length for 6 - 10 stitches per inch and attach the walking foot to sewing machine.
2. After pin-basting, decide which section of the quilt will have the longest continuous quilting line, oftentimes the area from center top to center bottom. Leaving the area exposed where you will place your first line of quilting, roll up each edge of the quilt to help reduce the bulk, keeping fabrics smooth. Smaller projects may not need to be rolled.
3. Start stitching at beginning of longest quilting line, using very short stitches for the first $1/4$" to "lock" beginning of quilting line. Stitch across project, using one hand on each side of the walking foot to slightly spread the fabric and to guide the fabric through the machine. Lock stitches at end of quilting line.
4. Continue machine quilting, stitching longer quilting lines first to stabilize the quilt before moving on to other areas.

Machine Stipple Quilting

The term, "stipple quilting," refers to dense quilting using a meandering line of machine stitching or closely spaced hand stitching.

1. Wind your sewing machine bobbin with general-purpose thread that matches the quilt backing. Do not use quilting thread. Thread the needle of your machine with transparent monofilament thread if you want your quilting to blend with your quilt top fabrics. Use decorative thread, such as a metallic or contrasting-colored general-purpose thread, when you want the quilting lines to stand out more.
2. For random stipple quilting, use a darning foot, drop or cover feed dogs, and set stitch length at zero. Pull up bobbin thread and hold both thread ends while you stitch 2 or 3 stitches in place to lock thread. Cut threads near quilt surface. Place hands lightly on quilt on either side of darning foot.
3. Begin stitching in a meandering pattern *(Fig. 29)*, guiding the quilt with your hands. The object is to make stitches of similar length and to not sew over previous stitching lines. The movement of your hands is what determines the stitch length; it takes practice to coordinate your hand motions and the pressure you put on the foot pedal, so go slowly at first.

Fig. 29

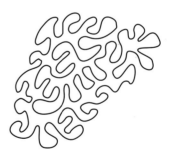

4. Continue machine quilting, filling in one open area of the quilt before moving on to another area, locking thread again at end of each line of stitching by sewing 2 or 3 stitches in place and trimming thread ends.

BINDING

Binding encloses the raw edges of your quilt. The instructions for each project provide the width and length of binding strip needed. The following instructions are for attaching French-fold binding with mitered corners.

1. Matching wrong sides and raw edges, press binding strip in half lengthwise to complete binding. Press 1 end of binding diagonally (*Fig. 30*).

Fig. 30

2. Beginning with pressed end several inches from a corner, lay binding around quilt to make sure that seams in binding will not end up at a corner. Adjust placement if necessary. Matching raw edges of binding to raw edge of quilt top, pin binding to right side of quilt along 1 edge.
3. When you reach the first corner, mark ¹/₄" from corner of quilt top (*Fig. 31*).

Fig. 31

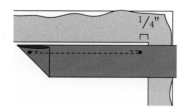

4. Using a ¹/₄" seam allowance, sew binding to quilt, backstitching at beginning of stitching and when you reach the mark (*Fig. 32*). Lift needle out of fabric and clip thread.

Fig. 32

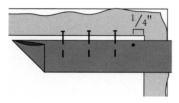

5. Fold binding as shown in *Figs. 33* and *34* and pin binding to adjacent side, matching raw edges. When you reach the next corner, mark ¹/₄" from edge of quilt top.

Fig. 33   *Fig. 34*

6. Backstitching at edge of quilt top, sew pinned binding to quilt (*Fig. 35*); backstitch when you reach the next mark. Lift needle out of fabric and clip thread.

Fig. 35

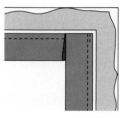

7. Repeat Steps 5 and 6 to continue sewing binding to quilt until binding overlaps beginning end by approximately 2". Trim excess binding.
8. If using 2¹/₂"-wide binding (finished size ¹/₂"), trim backing and batting a scant ¹/₄" larger than quilt top so that batting and backing will fill the binding when it is folded over to the quilt backing. If using narrower binding, trim backing and batting even with edges of quilt top.

9. On 1 edge of quilt, fold binding over to quilt backing and pin pressed edge in place, covering stitching line *(Fig. 36)*. On adjacent side, fold binding over, forming a mitered corner *(Fig. 37)*. Repeat to pin remainder of binding in place.

Fig. 36   *Fig. 37*

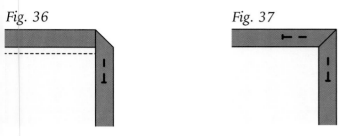

10. Blind Stitch binding to backing, taking care not to stitch through to front of quilt. To Blind Stitch, come up at 1, go down at 2, and come up at 3 *(Fig. 38)*. Length of stitches may be varied as desired.

Fig. 38

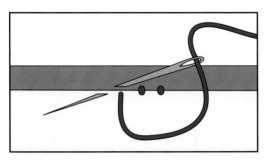

ADDING A HANGING SLEEVE

Attaching a hanging sleeve to the back of your wall hanging or quilt before the binding is added will allow you to use a dowel rod or wooden slat to display your completed project on a wall.

1. Measure the width of the wall hanging and subtract 1". Cut a piece of fabric 7"w by the determined measurement.
2. Press short edges of fabric piece ¼" to wrong side twice; machine stitch in place.
3. Matching wrong sides, fold piece in half lengthwise to form a tube.
4. Matching raw edges, baste hanging sleeve to center top edge on back of quilt.
5. Bind quilt as indicated in project instructions, treating the hanging sleeve as part of the backing.
6. Blindstitch bottom of hanging sleeve in place, taking care not to stitch through to front of quilt.
7. Insert rod or slat into hanging sleeve.

SIGNING AND DATING YOUR QUILT

Your completed quilt is a work of art and should be signed and dated. There are many different ways to do this, and you should pick a method that reflects the style of the quilt, the occasion for which it was made, and your own particular talents. The following suggestions may give you an idea for recording the history of your quilt for future generations.

- Embroider your name, the date, and any additional information on the quilt top or backing. You may choose embroidery floss colors that closely match the fabric you are working on, such as white floss on a white border, or contrasting colors may be used.
- Make a label from muslin and use a permanent marker to write your information. Your label may be as plain or as fancy as you wish. Stitch the label to the back of the quilt.
- Chart a cross-stitch label design that includes the information you wish and stitch it in colors that complement the quilt. Stitch the finished label to the quilt backing.

Metric Conversion Chart

Inches x 2.54 = centimeters (cm)	Yards x .9144 = meters (m)
Inches x 25.4 = millimeters (mm)	Yards x 91.44 = centimeters (cm)
Inches x .0254 = meters (m)	Centimeters x .3937 = inches (")
	Meters x 1.0936 = yards (yd)

Standard Equivalents

⅛"	3.2 mm	0.32 cm	⅛ yard	11.43 cm	0.11 m
¼"	6.35 mm	0.635 cm	¼ yard	22.86 cm	0.23 m
⅜"	9.5 mm	0.95 cm	⅜ yard	34.29 cm	0.34 m
½"	12.7 mm	1.27 cm	½ yard	45.72 cm	0.46 m
⅝"	15.9 mm	1.59 cm	⅝ yard	57.15 cm	0.57 m
¾"	19.1 mm	1.91 cm	¾ yard	68.58 cm	0.69 m
⅞"	22.2 mm	2.22 cm	⅞ yard	80 cm	0.8 m
1 "	25.4 mm	2.54 cm	1 yard	91.44 cm	0.91 m